Wishing My
Father Well

Wishing My Father Well

A Memoir of Fathers, Sons, and Fly-Fishing

William Plummer

THE OVERLOOK PRESS
WOODSTOCK & NEW YORK

First published in the United States in 2000 by
The Overlook Press, Peter Mayer Publishers, Inc.
Lewis Hollow Road
Woodstock, New York 12498
www.overlookpress.com

Library of Congress Cataloging-in-Publication Data

Plummer, William, 1945–
Wishing my father well : a memoir of fathers, sons, and fly-fishing /
William Plummer.
p.   cm.
1. Fathers and sons—United States—Case studies. 2. Plummer,
William, 1945– 3. Fly-fishing—New Jersey. I. Title.
HQ756.P59   2000   306.874'2—dc21   00-025298

Book design and type formatting by Bernard Schleifer
Manufactured in the United States of America
FIRST EDITION
1 3 5 7 9 8 6 4 2
ISBN 1-58567-031-6

For Ger

ACKNOWLEDGMENTS

I want to thank three special people who encouraged me during the writing of this book: Dave Grogan, Dan Green, and Nick Lyons. I want to thank Peter Mayer and the staff at The Overlook Press—and the members of Anglers Anonymous. Finally, and above all, I want to thank Mary Suzanne Huzinec.

. . . just a toast to trout men, one and all. There are so few left, so few who believe the earth is enough.

—HARRY MIDDLETON, *The Earth Is Enough*

Life is lived forward, learned backward.

—SØREN KIERKEGAARD

Prologue

I HEAR THE STREAM before I see it. I hear it swirling and clattering through the stand of hardwoods at the far end of the cornfield, as I trip across the rock-hard furrows in my waders. As always, I feel a rush of my own.

I enter the little woods and stoop to examine a skunk cabbage. It's early March and there is still snow on the ground here but, like me, the skunk cabbage is pushing the season. Mottled with maroon, shaped like a flame, it has burned its way up through the frozen earth, leaving a ring of wet. I peel back the fibrous hood and discover a tiny fist of yellow-green blossoms and an overwintering fly.

In a few weeks the grove will be crawling with wildflowers. Trout lillies and hepatica, then rue anemone, spring beauties, assorted phlox, violets in blue and white. But poking around, I can find no other early risers, not even the first shoots of the marsh marigold that rooted last year in the rich black muck behind the big old sycamore.

The woods appear to catch on fire as a band of red-winged blackbirds scorches by, their epaulets bright as coals. It's the time of year when the red-winged males put on their air show. I watch one land on a low-slung branch and knock a rival for a squawking loop, then listen as he blows up like a balloon and crows about his badass self.

I know what I'm doing, dawdling here. It's an old monk's trick, a strategy of self-denial. I'm sharpening the edge of a coming pleasure by postponing its thrust. Then again, maybe it's disappointment I'm delaying. Eventually, I know, I'm going to have to take a look at the river.

Might as well be now, I think, as I push through the curtain of willows and alders and get my first view of the water since the late fall. Each year I worry that the stream will go through something over the winter, and I won't know about it until I show up again in the spring. But I see with relief—I realize, suddenly, I've been holding my breath—that everything is pretty much as I left it. It's the same South Branch of the Raritan that I've come to know, and rely on, for going on six years. It's the same stream my father knew and fished for most of his life.

The South Branch is swollen but running clear. It has been a tough winter with serious snowfall. I can see where the torrent climbed the banks and ripped new paths through the brush. Some of the smaller smooth-barked trees are still coated with mud halfway up their trunks. A skil saw, a Black & Decker, washed from somewhere up above, sits in a small clearing, its short thick electrical cord curled beside it. And tatters of white plastic bags hang from the bushes like tiny flags of surrender.

But the long riffle, where the trout get so dense on certain muggy June nights that you can comb them like hair, it's still there. So are the rocks at the head of the pool, a tonsillar pair straddling the throat, the bigger one trailing a ribbon of gently coptering water that almost always yields a decent brown. So too are the big willows on the far bank, although the last in the sequence has been felled by a winter storm and lies partly submerged. Tough for the willow, but good for the fisherman. It's what is called a "sweeper," a new neighborhood for trout.

I ease down to the bottom of the pool and sit on a rock. I think how Dad would have fished this water, and just like that, his image bodies up as if from the element itself. My father was different from me, physically (and in every other way, I once mistakenly believed). He was short and broad and meaty across the chest, a powerful man with legs that became increasingly bird-like as he aged. In my reverie, he is dressed in cheap canvas waders that are patched with chunks of rubber cut from a bicycle tire inner tube, and his favorite beige fishing jacket, topped off with that funny green felt hat that covered his bald spots. He is standing in nearly waist-high water, and he is casting directly upstream, fingering back the line as it drifts glacially toward him.

My father is working beneath the surface. He is fishing a nymph, a tiny bit of fur and feather that imitates an immature aquatic insect, which may have lost its grip on the rocky stream bottom and is caught in a liquid free fall, or which is in the midst of hatching, of rising to the surface where it will struggle to climb out of its shuck, spread its wings and fly into the trees. For the most part, trout accept nymphs lightly. In fact, there is no sure way to tell if a trout has taken a nymph. Sometimes, if you are lucky, the line will jog back upstream; other times it will stop or hesitate. Often, the line will do nothing at all.

And yet my father is fishing his fly, or artificial, without a strike indicator—that is, without one of those bright plastic bobbers that you see on every stream today and that take much of the mystery out of nymphing. Dad may have greased his line, so that it rides high in the water. Or he may have run his thumbnail along the butt section of his leader and put a crick in it, so he can see if it straightens out and judge that a trout is fooling with his fly. But that's as far as he will go to give himself an advantage.

My father is not a purist, but a dinosaur. He simply fishes the way he learned to growing up on New Jersey's obscure little trout streams. He fishes with the techniques he gleaned from the older boys, from the outdoor magazines, and, mostly, from his own experience. Nymphing, I believe, spoke directly to who and what my father was.

It is a blue collar, lunch pail kind of fly-fishing, a scant step up, in the minds of the real purists, from drowning worms. It looks especially pallid when compared to dry fly-fishing. In the proper hands, angling with a dry fly is a thing of beauty. It tests a near-athletic ability to cast an artificial forty, fifty, seventy feet through the air and set it delicately, tantalizingly, down before a feeding trout. Nymphs, by contrast, are mostly fished with a short line and often with clunky bits of tin or lead to sink the artificial to the bottom of the stream. You don't have to be a maestro with the fly rod to fish a nymph.

A nymph fisherman works beneath the surface for prey he does not see. He does not observe the take, but infers it from a number of clues, most of which, should you ask him, he cannot adequately describe or explain. The truth is, a nympher angles with his nerves. His fishing is less a matter of skill than of sensibility, maybe even of soul. A nymph fisherman is, almost literally, a deeper person, someone who sees things that are not there.

I am mulling these thoughts on an early March morning while sitting on the rock at the bottom of the cornfield pool, and they broaden out like the tongue of current that thrusts down from the riffle above. I think how it took me years to recognize my father's depths, how I am sounding them still. I think how all I ever saw, growing up, was his difference from me, how everything always seemed to come between us—my long hair, the Vietnam War, his temper, my temper, our layered relationship to my mother. I think how for years, decades really, my father, a nymph fisherman who communicated better with trout than human beings, must have stood on the periphery of my life, not knowing how to get in. . . .

But the reverie is taking me places I don't want to go to right now. It is a warm almost-spring day, after a long hard winter, and I have come here to fish.

One

MY FISHING LIFE did not begin in childhood, as it does with most people. It began with my father's death, although I didn't realize it at the time. I was too busy trying to deal with the mess I had made of my old life.

I was in London with Nicky when the call came about Dad. Nicky and I were still getting used to the difference in time, and it seemed as if we had just put our heads down to sleep, when we were roused by our host at 6 A.M. I staggered out to the hall to hear my sister Kappy's voice.

"Billy," she said through tears, "I know you just got there. But you have got to come home. . . ."

I had brought my ten-year-old son to London as a gesture—of what exactly, I did not really know. I was crashing around in the dark. I had just left Nicky's mother, and the only thing I knew for certain was that I had to tell my little boy, in some dramatic way short of hiring a skywriter, that I still loved him, and I was not about to dump him too.

Samantha, his three-year-old sister, I figured, was still too young to understand.

Nicky and I had spent the day bouncing from the Tower of London to Harrods to the museums on Exhibition Road. We must have looked like father and son on holiday. But even cursory inspection would have shown that our euphoria was fueled by desperation. At some level we knew if we could just keep filling up on museums, we would not have to face the fear and emptiness we felt.

It was a difficult time for everyone, but especially for Nick, who had had his own recent brush with mortality. Some weeks earlier, Nicky had been swiped by a speeding motorist as he stepped off the curb in front of our house in New Jersey to cross for the school bus. I was on the third floor, trying to write. I had no view of the street. But I heard the tires. I'll never forget the way every other concern in my life ceased to exist—my dying marriage, my dying career (the book I'd spent six years on had just been published to general indifference)—the way my entire being strung tight as a wire toward the street. Finally, I heard Molly cry out below: "God, it's Nicky!"

I took the stairs two and three at a time and was already raving when I went through the front door. I careered out into the yard, past the big silver beech, looking for someone, anyone at all, to hit.

"Hey, take it easy! It wasn't us," said two husky young men—painters working in the neighborhood—who dodged my charge as they came up the walk.

Then: "He's okay. Really, your boy is okay."

I looked over at the curb, where Nicky was lying in his mother's lap. He was scared but not seriously hurt—he had a gash over his left eye—and he was sobbing with his whole body. The driver of the school bus was on one side of Molly; behind him, the entire shipment of kids pressed up against the windows. On the other side, carefully picking his way toward me, was the guy who had hit my son. Hardly the arch-fiend I had hoped for, he was a slight Asian man with what looked like a stenciled-on mustache.

"Please," he implored, "I don't see the boy. The bus don't put on the lights. Please, I also have son."

Still marinating in anger about Nicky, about my toilet of a life, I ignored the poor guy.

Fuck him, I remember thinking. Let him twist.

When I finished talking long distance with my sister, I went back to the bedroom and got in with Nick. I put my arms around him and pulled him close. I told him that his grandfather, whom he called Deggie, had had a heart attack while fishing and just sat back on the bank and expired.

I started to mouth the sentiment that would become a mantra with my parents' friends—that Dad's death could not have been better scripted by the movies, that he died with his boots on, doing the thing he loved best.

But Nicky cut right through the B.S.

"Was Deggie all alone?" Nicky asked.

"I don't know," I said. Then, with a shudder: "Yes, I think he was. I think you always are."

* * *

A few days later, there was a memorial service on the long green lawn that swept past my parents' house in western New Jersey. A large, rambling clapboard and fieldstone affair, the house had been an eighteenth-century inn. It banked on a hill and looked out on four woodsy acres that melted into a forest. Deer often came down to drink in the pond and chew on the ornamental evergreens.

I spoke at the service. I alluded to the problems my father and I had when I was a kid. Mostly I spoke about how I had come to appreciate him, and about how different he was from my mother (or Ger, as I had called her since I was a teen). Where Ger was wind and fire, Dad was the earth itself; he was some-one who had to be unearthed, for his riches did not lie on the surface. I spoke about how he was someone you spent an evening with in a quiet corner at a party or went on walks with. How he knew the names of trees, recognized animal tracks in the dirt or snow, could think like a fish. How he was also a reader, someone who got hold of a book and did not let go until he drained it. And Lord help you if you were "flowery," about the worst thing he would say about a writer or, for that matter, about a person. . . .

Afterward, I hid in the kitchen and got into the scotch. I felt as though I had exposed myself—and, in the process, had not told the truth. Not the whole truth, anyway. My eulogy suggested that I had reached some kind of peace with my father, and I knew that I hadn't.

I didn't want to talk to anyone. But I must have ended up conversing with a dozen people who both-ered to hunt me down. Most of these were clients. My father had spent the last twenty-five years of his life restoring antique furniture, and person after person wanted to tell me how he had made them a table out of beat-up old boards or had turned their mutilated bureau into an *objet* of museum quality.

But the one I will always remember was the younger brother of one of Dad's childhood friends, a man I hardly knew and had not seen for decades.

"Do you fish?" he asked me.

"A little," I said. "No, not really."

He seemed surprised, disappointed.

"Well," he said, "I'm going to tell you this anyway, because it might mean something to you some day." He paused and looked at me intently. "Your father was a nymph fisherman. He was closer to nature than the rest of us."

A couple of weeks after the cremation, my mother, my nephew, and I took on the barn. A red prefabricated metal structure, the barn sat above my parents' house and was the hub of Dad's business. It was a big step up from the old chicken coops where he used to operate and probably would have kept on operating if they hadn't burned down.

That Sunday we arrived after the fire had been put out. I will never forget the mess: the tangle of wood and metal smoldering on the wet concrete floor; the volunteer firemen in their slickers, still buzzing with excitement; my father, his eyes dull with despair, foraging in the slop for tools that had survived the blaze and could somehow still be used.

It was my mother, as always, who fetched my

father from the ashes—and now, six years later, she was trying to do the same for herself. The trick, she knew, was to stay busy. Tackle the barn. Sort through the sea of tables and chairs, bureaus and bedsteads. Cull the unfinished pieces that belonged to customers and ferry them back home.

I had braced myself for an ordeal. But the whole business proved to be surprisingly painless. There were no tears or tirades. Quite the opposite. My mother was her usual incandescent self. If anything, she was turned up a notch, almost giddy with grief.

"He's been working on this for days," she said gayly, caressing a battered highboy—using, I could not help but notice, a verb tense that allowed my father a future.

For weeks we circled the wagons around her.

My mother tried to put up a brave front, but she was too mercurial to sustain it. She was okay at work, which she went back to almost right away. The hard part was coming home. She'd sit in the driveway, with her little black poodle, unable to get out of the car. My sister Kappy would find her there an hour later, waiting for Dad to come down from his barn and greet her, as he had each night of their lives.

The gestural, ritual cocoon of life was torn, and there was no thread to mend it. My mother had never spent a night alone in her life and she was not about to start now. My two sisters, Sam, Nicky, and I and a host of relations took turns sleeping in the adjoining bed. But even our rotating guard failed to make her feel safe. We had locks installed on both sets of doors leading to my mother's bedroom. But they offered her little comfort. It was somewhat like stretching a grate across an abyss: she might not fall in, but she could still look down into it.

Over the next few months, my family went through the familiar stages of grief, cycling back and forth along the axis of denial and despair. Eventually, though, it hit—and lingered—on a stage that I suspect will not be found in most of the handbooks on dealing with such a loss.

We had each, it turned out, been haunted by the same dark thought—that my father had not died as the men at his fishing club said he did. That he did not simply feel pain in his chest, lie back on the nearest bank, and go gentle into the night. Our fear was that he had drowned. No one dared express this, out of concern for the others. No one, that is, but my irrepressible mother. Each night in her dreams, she saw Dad lying face down in a swimming pool, like William Holden in *Sunset Boulevard*.

Gradually, mercifully, Ger's dreams were re-colorized and my father experienced a sea change into something rich and strange. He became, I gathered, a kind of familiar spirit, easily dialed up and always willing to help my mother realize some elusive end. At one point, he was working at fixing up my sister Melissa with one of my childhood buddies, who was still gimpy from divorce.

I was incredulous, but kept my mouth shut.

A good thing, too, because Ger's dreams quickly infected everyone. Soon everyone was seeing my father and not just when they tucked in at night. It was as if my entire family had been been abducted by Gabriel García Márquez. Kappy saw Dad one afternoon jogging down from his barn. He was wearing the heavy brown canvas coat that he worked in during the winter, never mind that the temperature was well into the eighties. Melissa saw him in the kitchen, his arm wrapped around Ger.

Meanwhile, up in the barn, the fey Puerto Rican floral designer who'd just encamped felt compelled to paint a fully-armed angel on the door to hold my father at bay. Milagro, his buxom female assistant, complained that Dad was "getting fresh. He keep untying my shoe."

Mostly, I was amused, until Huey, the young lady from work I had been pursuing, seemed to join the chorus. Huey and I were in Montreal, where I was playing in a hockey tournament with some other bozos with little hair and less sense. Huey mentioned that she'd lit a candle for Dad that morning at the cathedral. It stopped me in my tracks.

"Why?" I asked, unaccountably annoyed.

"To wish him well," she said.

"What do you mean 'to wish him well'?" I snapped. "He's *dead*. Don't you people realize that?"

Two

A FEW DAYS LATER, I got into my Subaru Justy—the tin-can-of-a-car that was the spoil of my pending divorce—and drove out to the South Branch of the Raritan River. The South Branch was Dad's home water. But I was not a member of his angling club, and would be poaching if I fished there, so I resorted to an artificials-only section ten miles below known to local anglers as the Gorge.

I bounced along the dirt road that ran beside the stream for better than a mile, looking for the ideal spot, one where, with my slender casting talent, I would not be quite so likely to decorate the trees. turned into a little parking lot next to an open reach of water and walked down to the end of a long and, I thought, fishy-looking pool.

I joined the eight-foot graphite rod, worked the line through the guides, and attached a leader. Then I sat down and tried to purge my mind of everything but the scene before me. If you did so, Dad used to say, the stream would disclose itself.

But my mind per usual had a mind of its own.

* * *

It was funny, but I could hardly remember my father fishing with me when I was a kid, except for a few times on the Rahway, which wound through Cranford, the Jersey town where I grew up. The Rahway didn't count. It was carp factory even then.

I remembered Dad teaching me how to catch night crawlers. How we would hose down the walk that skirted our backyard, come back at night with a flashlight that had a piece of red cellophane taped across the beam, and discover them wriggling on the bricks. I remembered, as an even younger kid, sitting downstairs in the basement and opening up the long cardboard cylinders that housed his bamboo rods. I would remove the rods from their cloth sheathings and join them together. Imitating my father, I'd roll the nickel silver male tube of the ferrule in the crease beside my nose to pick up that bit of lubricating oil. Then I'd push the male spike in and out of the female; over and over I would do this, strangely gratified by the popping sound it made.

I remembered casting sessions in the backyard— the goal being to drop the end of the line and leader in the shell-shaped cement birdbath. And I remembered watching Dad tie flies, which he did by the hour in a tiny basement alcove hemmed by pipes, and marveling at the materials he used—the oily rooster necks, long wands of peacock tail, and cotton candy tufts of polar bear hair. I even remembered tying a doorstop of a streamer under his gaze.

But I could not remember going with him, just the two of us, on an expedition to one of the state's better streams, the Pequest maybe or the Flatbrook.

In part, I assume that we rarely went fishing together because he had no time. When I was a kid he always worked on Saturdays in my grandfather's (my mother's father's) custom shoe store in New York. I suspect, too, that fishing was a release for him, and I—feeding me, trying to get ahead for me—was part of the galaxy of pressures from which he needed release. I also think that my father did not fish with me because it was assumed that I was not really suited for it. Every family has its myths, which create their own invidious truths. The one about me was that I was inept in manual matters, that I could not drive a nail without retooling my thumb. Never mind that I had excellent hand-eye coordination and was one of the best athletes in my school. My mother, I believe, stood somewhere in the shadows behind this myth. Ger had hopes for me. She wanted me to be someone who used his brains, not his hands.

Then, there's the fact that Dad and I were mostly lost to each other during my long adolescence. For years, I can see now, I was too angry at him to let him into my life. I was repelled by what I took to be his relationship with my mother and the way that relationship leaned on me.

My mother and father married young, although not so young for their day. She was nineteen and he was twenty-one. But everything was accelerated by World War II, when there was little time for lovers to truly get to know each other.

My parents must have thought they had that covered. They had both grown up, after all, in Cranford, and my mother's older brother had been one of Dad's fishing and camping buddies. But my parents did not really know each other. All they had to go on—my mother, I think, especially—were glossy projections of youthful desire.

In my mother's eyes, my father was a romantic figure. He came from dour, hard-working Presbyterians who were as close with their emotions as they were with a buck. But that isn't what Geraldine Vogel saw when she looked at Bill Plummer. She saw the handsome son of the town's first family—part of Cranford was built on what had once been Plummer land—with athletic ability and an aw-shucks, Gary Cooper manner. She saw the young man her older brother looked up to.

My mother is the child of an alcoholic. It may be the central fact of her life. She is the spawn of a man who, when in his cups, took savage pleasure in cutting her down, in ridiculing everything about her, especially that quality that made her who she is: her special vividness. He called her "codfish mouth" because she supposedly talked too much.

I adored this man, my grandfather. But by the time I came along he was drinking Near beer. Kid, as I called him, was still a great, roaring, leonine presence. I can imagine what he was like when he was running on alcohol. But my mother did not fold under his abuse. It merely concentrated her intentions. It made her hungry to succeed, to prove that she was a person of consequence.

If Ger had been born twenty years later, she would have sought success on her own. But she was a creature of her time and milieu and was schooled to put her hopes in a man. The trouble was: she picked the wrong man. Or, rather, the man she picked was not the man she thought he was.

My father could not even bring himself to ask my mother out on their first date. It was the summer of 1941, and they were down on the Jersey shore. Dad sent Rhys Stanger, one of his buddies, to my mother's place to ask her out for him. Ger said yes with alacrity, but wondered why my father didn't come by and ask her himself.

"Oh, he's busy," said Rhys.

"Doing what?" my mother asked.

"Shaving," said Rhys.

I have heard this story told any number of times, and always humorously. But it has its ominous aspect. The fact is: my father was a preternaturally private person with little social confidence.

My father got news of my birth while stationed off Iwo Jima. He was the executive officer on a sub-chaser, one of those wood-hulled tubs used to mark off landing corridors during amphibious invasions. A ship pulled up beside my father's and a sailor sang out, "Congratulations, Mr. Plummer, you are the father of a son, William Halsey Jr." It would be nine months before he saw me.

In the interim, my mother would try to make up for his absence by speaking to me in a gruff voice and throwing me hard onto the bed. She would even put me on top of the fridge and walk into the next room, saying that she would be back in a while—this in a curious attempt to make me tough.

My father was damned if I would grow up a sissy. He was apoplectic when he came home from working in New York one day to discover that my mother had dolled me up in a pink suit from Best & Co. On another occasion, when my mother suggested that I be known by my middle name, Halsey, my father countered: "You might as well call him Abercrombie and completely do him in!"

This is another humorous family story, but it too is telling. My mother wanted to call me by my middle name because it sounded, to her ear—that of the daughter of a first generation German-American shoemaker—like something the Astors, say, might name a kid. My father rejected the name because it struck him as phony. Because his family practically dated back to Plymouth Rock, and he didn't care about all that crap, anyway.

And so their pattern was set.

My mother did everything she could to elevate the family and to demonstrate our good breeding, despite our limited means. She was determined that I go to nursery school with the better-heeled toddlers in Cranford. When my father said that there was no money for it, Ger covered my tuition by picking up some of the other kids en route and taxiing them to the school as well.

Next, she decided that I would go to Pingry, the tony boy's day school in our area. Again she was undaunted by Dad's pocketbook realism. She wangled me a full scholarship, largely, I think, by charming my father's big-hearted, blue-blooded cousin, who was a school trustee.

My mother was determined that her children would not be shortchanged by life. She saw to it that we belonged to a swimming and tennis club that was frequented by the top families in the county (she worked in a women's dress shop to foot this bill). She saw to it that I took ballroom dancing lessons (she pitched in as a chaperone), that my drawers were filled with Oxford cloth shirts monogrammed with my initials (never mind that the shirts were from a discount department store in Newark), that I had a tuxedo for the debutante parties and went to Bermuda for spring break with my rich classmates (even though Dad was out of work).

There is a sense in which my mother, like Jay Gatsby, sprang from her own "Platonic conception" of herself. She believed in Gatsby's green light, that a person can invent and reinvent himself; all you need is motivation and willpower. My mother, in short, believed in the American Dream.

So, I think, did my father. But he staked out a radically different corner of it. Dad's American Dream was to be left alone. It was first dreamed into being by his forbears, the Pilgrim fathers, who came to the New World to avoid persecution in England and have things their own way.

My father was, at heart, a Puritan. I don't mean by this that he was a prude or a killjoy, far from it. My father laughed easily and heartily and could be quite bawdy. I mean rather that he was steeped in his Calvinist heritage.

Deep down, my father was a fatalist. He was of the mind-set that holds that some souls are saved and some are abandoned, and there's no way of knowing which fate is yours; nor is there anything much you can do about it. What you can do is lead a sober, frugal, self-reliant life. You can pour yourself into work—not with any ulterior motive, not to build a career, not to amass a fortune or rise in society—because work confers on your life a kind of sanctity, because diligence in work is evidence of grace.

My parents' dreams were wildly at odds. For years, though, it wasn't that obvious because Dad went through the motions of being upwardly mobile. Then, about fifteen years into their union, he hit a wall. He stopped working in my grandfather's custom shoe business and entered the corporate world. He was fired from job after job. At one point, Dad was unemployed for a year and was so distraught that my mother came home one day to discover him hiding in a closet, crying.

Eventually, my father found his path. He converted his weekend hobby of restoring antique furniture into a modest living. Eventually, my mother found a way to channel her own craving for success, her need to disprove my grandfather's claim that she was nothing and always would be. She opened a gift and antique store that became a mecca for the smartest people in the area, and she poured her aspirations into her children and grandchildren.

But for years my mother's disappointment was registered in one-sided quarrels. I was too young to understand what was really going on. I was too young to see, much less comprehend, the collision of dreams. I could only see that my father, who was unskilled in argument, was absorbing a beating.

Memory is a curious thing. It is not interested in number but in weight. It seizes upon certain images and ignores the rest though, statistically, they may be more significant. This is to say: I don't know how often my parents actually fought. But in my memory, my father is cowering in the kitchen. He is on the fringe of the room, backed up against the china cupboard, and he is trying to fend my mother off with lame bits of sarcasm. "That's good, Ger, *really* good. Is that the best you can do?" I hear him saying, with this tight little grin on his face. In the severity of youth, I wrote him off as a weakling.

In the decade or so before his death, Dad began to court me. I don't know why he did this. Maybe he sensed that we could not continue to tiptoe around each other forever. Maybe he saw that everything was at last equal between us: I had my own troubled marriage and often heartbreaking relationship with my son. Whatever the case, the stars were finally aligned. We had another chance.

It was a slow, diffident campaign my father waged, as if he were a suitor fearful of rejection. It was supremely touching. This man who used to ask my mother, "How's Bill doing?" started to call me himself. He called the first time after I had broken my shoulder playing hockey. He wanted to make sure I was healing; that was the excuse.

Once the way was cleared, he called every Thursday afternoon. (I know the time with my nerves, because I still half expect to hear the phone ring.) He did his best to keep up with me, asking after the book that had me closeted and even feigning an interest in the subject, boxing. He not only inquired after my world; he invited me into his, which was largely defined by fly fishing for trout.

He had tried several times before to get me interested. But this time he went for broke. He bought me Red Ball waders and a Courtland vest; he built me a rod, tied me up some flies and leaders.

We went over to his club, where he stood patiently at my side and waited for something to applaud. Knee-deep in water, we plied a nymph through every hot spot on the stream, including places where, I know now, the fish will sometimes almost hook themselves—with no luck.

Within an hour, my back was aching and I was dying of boredom. Within two hours we were in a nearby tavern, where I bent my elbow to better effect.

After a while, I got up from the log—and my musings on Dad and my childhood—and started fishing the Gorge.

It was almost noon. I kept expecting other anglers to show up, but surely they knew better. It was the middle of the day in the middle of July, and the sun was drilling holes in the water. Forget about feeding, the fish were just trying to survive. The chances are that the trout were not even in the long, languid stretch of the South Branch that I had chosen to belabor, but were queued up at invisible springs trying to suck oxygen out of the icy infusion.

I opened my father's nymph box and considered the possibilities. I settled on the biggest fly in there, theorizing that the bigger the artificial, the more irresistible it had to be to the trout. Then I set about trying to attach it to the leader. The only fishing knot I knew was the (un)improved clinch knot, and it took me several minutes to effect it.

On my first cast I caught the tree behind me. I had been so intent on casting I forgot it was there. I gave a tug on the line, hoping the fly would pull free. I tugged again, harder, and the knot unraveled, leaving the artificial in the tree. No big deal, I thought. There were lots more in my father's box.

This time I picked a fuzzy brown nymph with gold wire around the middle and spent close to fifteen minutes putting it on. The tying end of the leader had curled up like a pig's tail, and I didn't know enough to snip it.

I walked into the water again. Mindful of the tree, I sidearmed my backcast into a nest of stickers about thirty feet below me. I couldn't believe it. I gave a couple of tentative pulls on the line. Then I went over to the bank and sat down, fighting back tears. It didn't take much these days to get me going.

After a few minutes, I got up and peered into the briers. I couldn't see the fly, so I had no choice but to reach into the guts of the plant, to follow the line back into the maze—until, Shit! I cut myself. I was actually bleeding.

I threw down the rod and charged up the embankment to my car. I ripped open the hatch and pitched through the mound of books and clothes until I found a pair of leather-palmed driving gloves. I calmed down as I put them on. I walked slowly back to my rod, took a couple of deep breaths, and reached into the plant again. I began to disentangle the line, length by length, bit by bit.

It must have been ninety degrees out, and the stickers were biting through the wool part of the gloves. And then, as I wedged deeper into the shrub, they were biting through my shirt. I started to lose it. I gave up trying to coax the line out and found myself going toe-to-toe with the goddamn thing, pulling back on the line as hard as I could, when it suddenly came hurtling out, whipping me across the face and dumping me on my butt.

Just the line came out, though. The fly was gone. So was the leader. And so, what I noticed—once I stopped cursing and kicking the dirt—was the bright orange loop that my father had affixed to the end of the fly line. The loop was crucial, if you were going to use the loop-to-loop method of connecting the leader to the line. Or so I was told an hour later by the fellow in the fly shop that services the South Branch. The alternative to the loop, I gathered, was learning another wretched fishing knot.

"How do you put the thing on?" I asked him.

"There's nothing to it," he said. "Just read the instructions that come in the package."

Nothing to it, my ass. I spent three hours that night getting the loop onto my line. It works on the same principle as the novelty item known as the Chinese finger puzzle, the little woven deal that you slip onto your finger, then can't get off if you pull directly against it. The idea is to inch the woven tube at the end of the loop onto the end of the fly line. But try as I might, I could not get it to go on. Worse still, when I did manage to insert the line, just a millimeter, the weave of the tube would unravel into so much used dental floss.

Like everything else in fly-fishing, I was discovering, this business of the loop had the quality of ordeal about it. Around midnight, when I somehow managed to will the tube onto the line—and secured it with a small slip of red plastic—I felt as though I had slain the Nemean lion or cleansed the Augean stable and was due some kind of cosmic reward. For starters, a trout or two.

Three days in a row I piled into my Justy—or "clown car," as Nicky called it—and made the hour-long trek to the South Branch, where I continued to get my hooks into everything but trout. I became especially adept at the "two-fer": hooking the bottom of the river first, then, in an effort to free it, jacking the fly up over my head into a waiting tree. I hooked everything in sight, and many things that were not in sight, until I hooked them.

I hooked every bit of my clothing, including my waders. In a moment of thoughtless anger (versus the other, contemplative kind), I plucked the fly from my canvassed leg, leaving a tiny hole that I discovered an hour later when my boot filled with water.

The third day was a Monday, and I played hooky from my job at *People* magazine, where I was a writer. After yet another afternoon of futility, I wandered into the fly shop where I'd purchased the loop and made the owner's day. He even called his mother in from the other room.

"You're not going to believe this," he told her. "This guy has been on the river three days in a row—at noon. He wants to know where the fish are!"

I thought about dropping him. But I was in dire need of information. After the hilarity died down, the shop owner told me there was some fishing on the South Branch, but it took place either very early in the morning or just before dark.

I returned to the Gorge that evening with $30 worth of new flies, including one, a dry fly called a Potamanthus, which made me think of an Indian chief.

This time there were cars in the roadside pull-offs.

The stretch I picked was already staked out by an older fellow, a fly-fishing dandy who might have leaped full-blown from the old Abercrombie and Fitch store window, complete with handlebar mustache and a red-and-white bandana at his throat. I didn't see him at first because I entered at the tail of the pool, and he was fifty yards upriver. He was actually in the run that fed into the riffles that dumped into the pool, not really in the same water at all. But I could tell that he pegged me for an intruder.

I watched the fellow, hoping to catch his eye and find out which way he was fishing, up or down, so I could point the other way. But he was busy pretending I didn't exist.

I was still debating what to do when the river wrested the decision from me. The South Branch, which had been as smooth as a freshly wiped bar, was suddenly littered with fish. Not only were trout erupting everywhere, but some sort of tiny bird was buzzing the length of the pool.

I hadn't a clue about what the trout were taking. In fact, I had no idea whether the food they were chasing was emerging from the water or landing on it. All I knew was that the fish were behaving as if I were part of the wallpaper. Within yards of me, they were vaulting two and three feet into the air.

I was reluctant to change flies, as it had taken forever to attach the artificial I had on. But after ten more precious minutes slipped by, I knew I had to give the Potamanthus a rest, especially after a six-inch trout nosed up beside it, gave it a sniff, and left it bobbing like a bath toy.

It didn't matter much what I put on next since I had no idea what I was doing. I thought I should stay with a dry fly. Beyond that, it was like going to the track for the first time and knowing nothing about the horses and being left to your hunches.

Looking up, after attaching a fluffy concoction called a Humpy, I saw that I no longer had the pool to myself. The dandy had eased down from above. Plus two more anglers, kids in their late teens, had arrived, moved in above me, and started bombing the water.

But nobody was catching anything, which was okay with me. It was even oddly reassuring. I had been catching nothing for days, and now I had company.

It also seemed to be okay with Beau Brummel, who positioned himself at the top of the pool and threw a long, elegant loop into our midst. He had his casting artistry to console him.

But it did not sit well with the late arrivals, who were, after all, teenagers. They changed flies the way they presumably did TV stations. Soon they had huge black streamers on their lines, and they were ripping them through the water as if they were spin-fishing.

I suppose it had to happen: they started snagging trout. The skinny kid with a band of acne below his turned-round baseball cap hooked the first one, in the back and probably by accident. But his pudgy friend, who quickly snagged another, clearly did it on purpose.

"No!" boomed the dandy. "You can't do that!"

I was outraged as well and was about to voice my own objection, when I hooked something myself. Only it wasn't a fish, and it wasn't in the water. It was one of those tiny birds making wild sorties through the dark sky. A bat, it turned out, when I reeled in.

"Cool, air fishing," said Pudgy. Then, splashing up beside me for a better look: "Can I have it?"

Three

A YEAR AND A HALF had passed since my father's death and I still could not get out of my own way. I was divorced, living alone in a garage apartment. Each day I seemed to set new lows for self-pity, and my temper was more trip wire than ever. Mostly, I was a danger to myself.

For five years I had coached my son's youth hockey league team and done pretty well at it. I don't mean that my kids always finished on top, but they would begin to get a glimmer of the valuable idea behind sports—that they pushed you to do things you never thought you could. My kids lost plenty of games, but always seemed to grow.

The parents were clearly aware of this. Alternately flattered and appalled, I would watch them pull strings so that their kids would play under me. But something happened over the previous year. Exactly what, I can't say. By most accounts, I lost my equilibrium. I apparently became so unstable, so bent on winning and likely to fly into a disproportionate rage, that the league disinvited me for the next season. I do remember telling one official to fuck himself, in front of a dozen wide-eyed children.

I also nearly got myself fired at *People*, where my job was to turn other people's reporting into finished articles. Deeply out of sorts, I hid in my office in the Time and Life Building and glowered at the editors when they came by with assignments.

I remember, during this period, asking to take the next week off, so I could fly to Costa Rica and hang with a pal who was writing a sea survival book. My editor conferred with his editor. Word came back that they couldn't spare me.

"If you had asked a week earlier," my editor said, "we could probably have found a way to—"

"Tough shit," I said. "I'm going."

And I did. I'm amazed they didn't can me.

Finally, several months later, fed up with my neo–Bartleby the Scrivener routine, the managing editor hauled me into his office and threatened me with something called "official warning."

"Why?" I had the stones to ask.

"Because," he said, "you're *disengaged*."

If only that had been true. If only I could have disengaged—from myself, the morass of me. But everywhere I went, I was there, the person I least wanted to be with.

Most of my life I've felt the pull of manic-depressive illness, which haunts my mother's family. I've done some reading on the subject and find that I mostly line up on the depressive side of the equation. This, in itself, is fairly depressing, although

I barely recognize the periods of pure listlessness some writers complain of—Ralph Waldo Emerson's going on in his essay "Experience" about his unshakable lethargy: "We are like millers on the lower level of a stream, when the factories above them have exhausted the water. We too fancy the upper people must have raised their dams." Or F. Scott Fitzgerald's talking in *The Crack-Up* about sleeping twenty hours a day and finding "every act of life from the morning toothbrush to the friend at dinner had become an effort."

I too found it hard to get started in the morning, but not because I was so exhausted I couldn't heft a toothbrush. Some mornings during the previous year, I simply could not get out of bed. I would lie there wide awake at dawn, having slept in fits or not at all during the night, and I would watch the first light creep in through the window. I would think that if I lay very still, if I made no effort to get up and did not so much as blink an eye or twitch a muscle, the day would not be able to begin. It would not know where to find me. Time would be forced to stand still.

The trouble was, I could not still my mind. I could not control my thoughts, which were not thoughts, really, but speeding cars through the brain. Then, after a while—after lying there, for God knows how long, being run over by my mind—I would begin to feel as though I could not move, that my staying in bed was no longer an act of will.

All my life I had lived with someone—with my parents while growing up, with roommates in college and while pursuing the single life in Manhattan, and then with Molly and the kids. The presence of other people, their noise and vitality, would get me up and moving in the morning. But living alone in my tiny garage apartment, I often didn't rise until noon, and then it was because the phone rang or someone banged on my door and broke the spell.

I had learned, when younger, to ride out the black moods. Even the blackest mood would eventually turn merely gray, and once it did, I found that I could often saddle up and kick it back to normal.

But none of the old devices seemed to work anymore, not in the old surefire way. There was ice hockey of course. But there was just so much hockey an allegedly grown man could play, and I was already doing it, when I could get it together, several nights a week. There was sex. But trial and a great deal of error suggested that sex brought with it at least as much baggage as it helped unload.

The truth is, I could not get seriously involved with a woman again for much the same reason I could no longer write—because I did not trust myself. Writing, meaningful writing, requires surrender to the imagination, a willingness to subject the self to ordeal with the genuine possibility of failure. "In the destructive element immerse," says Joseph Conrad in *Lord Jim*.

I no longer had the guts.

Then, one day my mother found Dad's fishing diary. It had been sitting for two years beside his ashes, which she kept in the den in an old pine box on top of the television. Ger must have put it there, whether consciously or not, for my father to take with him.

For surely there was fishing where he was going. Why else call it Paradise?

The diary was not much to look at—a six-hole loose-leaf binder, the size of a man's hand. The slick black cover was coated with a fine red-brown dust. Mahogany dust, most likely. Dad probably kept it in the barn, where everything was filmed with the by-product of the endless sanding.

I opened the binder with anticipation bordering on fear. I don't know what I expected to find inside. I knew that it would be about fishing, but I also knew that it was a diary—which is to say, private writing. I thought, and hoped, that it might open a window on my father's inner life. But there was more to it than that. Under the circumstances, these words came from beyond the grave, and I could not help thinking they were meant for me.

I told myself to take it slow, to savor each entry as I might a poem. But I soon realized that, far from being filled with poetic hints and lusters that could light up a hidden landscape, the diary was given over to the dull arithmetic of fly-fishing. Its eighty closely-written pages were a meticulous record of my father's last half-dozen seasons on the South Branch of the Raritan. Each dated entry was crammed with information about such matters as: the temperatures of the air and water; what insects my father saw and what artificials he used to try to effect a match; which ones took fish and which ones did not; and which ones he probably should have used.

The entries were models of economy, all stunted subjects and stranded predicates ("Went down to club, got there 6 P.M., road closed to lower stretch.

Fished down. Missed strike in Rope pool."). They were grouped tightly together, often two on a page, presumably so Dad could spot a trend and plan the day's campaign accordingly.

I read about a third of it, then, supremely disappointed, put it down. I found just one notation of a personal nature. At the end of the June 21, 1984 entry—during which he takes a dozen trout from six to sixteen inches and quits because it is "raining like hell"—my father writes, "Ack has cancer of the trachea." Ack was Bob Ackland, Dad's lifelong friend, who died a short time later. But that was as personal as my father was going to get.

A few days later, I picked up the fishing diary again and steeled myself to finishing it. This time I found several mentions of my own hapless hours on the trout stream. My father writes: "Caught or lost 15–20 browns & brooks between us. . . . Bill did well. Hope he gets to like it."

My father was being charitable. I may have lost a few trout, but I certainly didn't catch any. I would have remembered that. The next time out, on June 9 of that year, my father is reduced to saying, "Bill skittered nymph and good fish came after it. . . . Bill getting pretty good."

Two years later, on May 29, after another totally one-sided outing, my father takes solace in the comradery: "Wasn't good fishing. But enjoyed beers with Bill on way home."

I put the diary in the trunk at the foot of my bed, along with other keepsakes my mother had given me.

I pretty much forgot about it until a few months later, when one of Dad's friends from the club called and asked if I wanted to wet a line. It was October, and already raw outside.

I met Warren Radcliffe in Long Valley, where the club has a mile or so of prime water. Most of the members fished the pools by the clubhouse, which they stocked with monster trout you don't often see outside of New Zealand. "Pets," my father called them. He preferred the smaller, untutored native brooks and browns that teemed in the lower stretches, which is where Warren and I headed, beating our way through the waist-high grasses that retained just a faint memory of the fisherman's path.

Bald on top, with a prelate's fringe around the sides, Warren was, and is, a genial, sympathetic soul. His gentle speech and fine manners, though, conceal deeply-banked fires. In great shape for sixty, or even forty, he is a national squash champion and a successful dentist, although he was apparently no longer pleased about the latter. "Imagine working for thirty years and never seeing a happy face," said Warren, who mainly does root canals. "Imagine that everyone associates your face with pain."

I tried to imagine this, as we pressed on through the brush. Finally, we stepped through a hole in the willows and alders that gird the stream in the fishing club's lower venue.

"This is it, Stony Brook, your father's favorite pool," said Warren. "He used to stand there." Warren pointed to a large rock at the head of the pool.

I had been to Stony Brook before, but I'd never studied it. The brook itself spilled into the main flow about a hundred feet above; from there the stream, no more than twenty feet wide at that point, banged and slid past a procession of boulders, then gathered itself and raced across forty feet of cobbled bottom before plunging into the pool proper and fanning out. At the last second, the main thrust of the current veered away from my father's rock toward the far side, making the rock an ideal place from which to fish down into the guts of the pool.

"Once, I stayed in the bushes and watched your dad for about half an hour," said Warren. "He never once moved from his spot. He would throw his nymph up and across and follow it downstream with his rod, over and over. I think he caught three or four, just while I was watching him."

Warren left me and started fishing back the way we came. I could see him flicking his dry fly as he went. I just stood there, shivering in the cold.

Looking up through the trees that framed the sky, I saw a broad-winged bird swirling on a shaft of air. A hawk, I guessed. My father would have known what kind. I tried to remember what he had said about hawks, how they migrated in the fall when the temperature fell and the winds came in from the north. Or was it from the west?

I told myself there was no rush. I had all afternoon to fish. It would take Warren several hours to work his way back to the clubhouse. Then I opened up my fly box and searched for a particular pattern. I had consulted Dad's diary before leaving and zeroed in on an October entry in which he writes, "Small gray nymph's the ticket."

On my first cast, I hung up in the tree behind me. I could see the little bugger, dangling from a bough just overhead. I jumped up and tried to grab it, but it was too high and, in the process, one of my fly boxes popped out of an unzipped vest pocket and landed in the water.

I retrieved the box before it sank and drained it. Then I waded out of the stream and began to climb the tree, making use of the great tangle of roots that reared up and out from the eroded bank.

Almost immediately I felt a tug, as if someone had grabbed my vest from behind. My net, which hung down my back on a retractor, was stuck in a bush—and not just any bush, but one armed with stickers, which infiltrated the mesh, creating a sort of lumpy macrame. I attempted to weed them out but, after pricking my fingers, gave up and just snapped the stalks from the bush.

I gave up too on the idea of scaling the tree. I yanked on the line, hoping the fly would pull free. Instead, it broke off, leaving the fly and a third of the leader behind. Tears began to build behind my eyes as I searched the dripping box for another gray nymph.

This time, I shortened my casting stroke, sidearmed it up into the current. I followed the fly with my rod as it made its invisible journey down into the pool. I waited a few seconds for the nymph to complete its swing. Nothing.

Again and again I cast up into the fast water, with the same result. Then, finally, I felt something—

a slight but unmistakable weight on the line. I was so keyed up that I forgot everything Dad had told me, notably, "When you feel the take, lift the rod like you're answering the phone."

Instead, I ripped the rod into the air and, along with it, the clump of yellow leaves that I had hooked. I made a positive ID on the leaves as they billowed overhead and, with the remainder of the leader, wrapped several times around the bough of the demonic tree behind me.

I howled so loud the birds shot from the trees.

But my ineptitude proved to be providential. Once I got over feeling like Job, I was forced to put on a new leader. I attached the last gray nymph and cast it, as before, up into the current, only this time the taper was intact and the leader must not have seemed to the fish like a length of rope and it must have offered less resistance to the water and allowed the fly to sink to where the trout were holding, because I suddenly had one on the line.

He was a brook trout, no more than seven or eight inches long. But he was a beauty. It was spawning season, and my brookie was dressed to meet the ladies, with an orange sash along his pearl-white belly.

I held the tiny fish in my hand, and stared at him longer, I am sure, than I should have.

Then I let him go.

Four

THE NEXT SPRING I went up to the Orvis Company fly-fishing school in Vermont. Manchester is a storybook New England village with stately inns and elegant colonial homes with manicured properties. It calls to mind what Mark Twain, I think it was, said about the English countryside—that it was too pretty to be left out of doors. I put up at the Avalanche, a Motel 6–type establishment with a Chinese restaurant out past the outlet stores.

At Orvis, we took casting lessons by the pond that brimmed with hand-fed trout. We learned how bamboo rods are made and the virtues of weight-forward and double-tapered lines. There were lessons in entomology and the basic fly assortment, on knots and wading and leader design.

The instruction was well-intentioned and clearly presented. But it stayed with me about as long as the egg foo yung at the Avalanche. The problem was that I'd done little fishing as an adult and most of it just to be with Dad. I lacked the velcro of experience to make the information stick.

What I remember best about the school was the lifelong passion for fly-fishing of one instructor, who as a kid had gotten hold of several thirty-gallon aquariums and raised aquatic insects, so he could know what the trout knew. This same instructor had a five-pound brown living in the creek behind his house, but he said he had never angled for it. He thought of the trout as family.

I also remember the one afternoon of actual fishing. The staff took us down to the Battenkill and turned us loose on the river, each with a single artificial, a #14 Light Cahill dry fly. They told us to keep on fishing until we lost it.

I was determined to catch a trout, and even more determined not to lose the fly. I climbed at least one tree and a couple of times ventured out into waist-high water to unsnag it. Like most beginners, I was having a hard time seeing my fly on the water. Finally, I cast the Cahill into the foam line in the center of a run. I saw it briefly, then it vanished from view. I gave the line a tug, hoping to nudge the fly back into focus, and, to my surprise, tightened on a small but spectacularly exuberant brown trout.

I brought the fish in and learned the reason for its acrobatics. The hook was buried in its jaw. I was all over the poor thing trying to get the fly out, before it occurred to me to simply break it off. After all, I had caught my fish. I had proved, for the moment at least, that I was my father's son.

But I couldn't revive the trout. I held him in the shallows and moved him back and forth, forcing the water gently through his gills as the Orvis people had instructed. The trout would appear to be breathing on his own—I could see the little bellows going behind his head—and I'd release him and he'd look all right. Then the current would grab him and he'd spin down a chute and go belly up.

I must have tried to revive the little brown half a dozen times, each time crashing after him in my waders, growing more and more frantic. "Don't you die!" I shouted. "Don't you *dare* die!"

But he finally got away from me for good. The last time I chased him for fifty yards, hurdling rocks and deadfalls and ripping my waders, before giving up. I sat down on a log, stricken, for close to an hour. It was dark when I made my way back to my Justy, the lone car in the parking lot.

A few days later, I decided that the only way I was going to learn to fish was if I taught myself—with Dad's help.

My father's diary became for me a kind of Rosetta stone, a key to the languages of fly fishing. It was an almanac of sorts for the South Branch of the Raritan River. Instead of listing famous anniversaries and noting the phases of the moon, it charted the local insect hatches and effectively predicted how the fish would behave in relation to the vagaries of the weather and the progress of the seasons.

But there was more to the diary than mere practical information. Once I stopped faulting it for failing to reveal my father, I began to see that in its own way it did just that. It didn't tell me what I longed to know about his shrouded inner man. But it did offer glimpses of Dad simply being himself.

The diary contains bits of my father's humor, harvested as usual at his own expense. At one point, he writes of fishing on an overcast September day and catching a bunch of small brook and brown trout on tiny nymphs near the head of a pool. Then he spots "some heavy rises" down below. He gets out of the water and works up from the tail with a #18 Blue Wing Olive dry fly. "Hooked twenty-inch SUCKER," he writes with what I'm sure is a mixture of amazement—suckers *never* eat on the surface—and disgust at having to handle the slimy bottom feeder. "Fish I saw jumping were not trout but suckers. So am I."

The diary also gives a taste of Dad's irony, which was so lightly wrought and quietly offered that you had to pay attention to make it out at all. "Went to Stony Brook," he writes on June 1, 1986. "Beautiful day. Water at good level, good temp. But no hatch. Tried everything & caught only chub. Missed strikes on small Baetis nymph. Days like this Baetis nymph & B[lue] W[ing] O[live] dry have to be the answer. Fish moving occasionally & you can't see anything on the water. Just has to be a small dark fly."

Up to this point, this is a thoughtful rumination on a rare fishless day. But my father adds a tag line that turns the entry into a gentle critique of life and the expectations most of us generally can't help but bring to it. "Everything was perfect," he wryly concludes, "except the fish."

I went through the diary again and made a list of the

artificials he used on a regular basis. I broke them down into months and subdivided each month, in turn, into years. Thus in May 1980, the list shows Dad using, primarly, and in a range of sizes: a Black Gnat and a Dark Cahill wet fly; a Quill Gordon nymph and wet fly; a Hendrickson nymph; a March Brown nymph; a gray nymph; humpback nymphs in tan, gray, and green; Adams, Blue Wing Olive, and Light Cahill dries; as well as ant and beetle patterns. By 1987, his May repetoire also includes a red squirrel nymph, a peacock herl nymph, and a hare's ear nymph.

Compiling the list was complicated by the fact that my father was a fly tier and tended to identify his artificials by the materials he used, rather than by their popular names (the peacock herl nymph, for example, which, I suspect, was a Zug Bug). He was also a student of his stream, and many of his favorite imitations were his own confections.

Having the flies was one thing. Figuring out how to use them was another. The diary is riddled with clues, some of them tantalizing ("fish wanted a skipping fly"). But I was in need of more directed information, something closer to a how-to. I found it in Dad's compact fishing library.

Some of the books I had given him myself. These were coffee table-type volumes on casting and fly tying, which had come my way when I was a book review editor. But there was another, older, and well-thumbed set of books, including Ray Bergman's classic, *Trout*, the first fishing book my father ever owned. I inhaled these volumes, especially the pages on nymph and wet fly-fishing.

Nymphs, I gathered, could be fished at any level in the water column, and with a variety of techniques, depending upon where the insects were in the cycle of emergence. But such niceties were lost on me at the very beginning. Most of my early energies were taken up with a more basic problem—getting what Ray Bergman and the rest of the experts blithely refer to as a "natural drift."

For years I had simply cast my fly where my father suggested the trout might be and I had waited for the take, which, of course, never came. And with good reason, I was beginning to see. In my innocence, I had paid little attention to what the line was doing on the water, that is, to how the line was in relation to the flow of the stream.

Put simply, I didn't understand the job of the fly line. Or, rather, I didn't understand that the fly line really has two jobs to do. I knew that the line is the rocket, launched by the rod, which propels the almost weightless fly onto the water. But I didn't know that it is also the rudder that governs the float of the fly once it gets there.

Nor did I understand that the flow of a stream, which appears to be uniform, is actually made up of numerous individual currents, and that the line and the fly, when cast across a stream, are likely to be operating in different currents and, therefore, traveling at different speeds.

Thus I had little sense that, when the line is in a slow lane and the fly in a fast one, the line will cause the artificial to drag behind the other juicy-looking morsels that vie for the feeding trout's attention, and that the trout will therefore perceive this retard-of-an-imitation as anything but food. Nor did I realize that when the reverse is true—when the fast-moving line bellies out below the slow-moving artificial—the line will soon snap to attention and whip the fly around and most likely scare the fish.

I suspect that my father did not sit me down and explain the crucial theory of natural drift because he wanted to keep things simple. Because I was having enough trouble just keeping my fly out of the trees. Also, the problems of drift and drag, which are critical to all forms of fly-fishing, are not as obvious when you're fishing with nymphs because it's all going on beneath the surface.

Out of sight, I guess, out of mind.

That summer I played ice hockey late at night and saw, then stopped seeing, Huey, the young woman from work who would shuttle in and out of my life for several years. I also continued to fish the way my father had shown me. I cast the nymph down and across at about a forty-five degree angle and let it swing out below me. Only now I was aware of the play of the line and the importance of getting a drag-free float. I concentrated on the orange loop at the end of my line, which connnected to the loop of the leader. I watched that little orange flag like a hawk. I did whatever I could to make sure that it—and therefore the invisible fly and leader—traveled on the water at the same speed as the chunks of foam and debris bobbing around it.

I learned to keep as much of the line off the surface as possible. I learned to fish, when I could, with just a few feet of line and the nine-foot leader, which, being made of fine monofilament, cut right through the water. I contorted myself over the stream, extending the rod with one hand while holding onto a tree branch with the other. This was in an effort to keep the line off the surface and stave off drag, as I drifted the fly through a spot I was sure held a fish. Once I lost my grip and took a header.

Reading an article in one of Dad's fishing magazines, I got an idea. The article was about angling on a famous Montana trout stream. It told how the clients would cast their artificials from the guide boat and get what appeared to be an almost endless natural drift. The deal, as I understood it, was that the fishing guide would control the speed of the boat so that the boat moved at pretty much the same rate as the current that held the target trout.

There are places in the Gorge where the flow concentrates into a strip maybe twenty- to thirty-feet wide and the water is abutted by a mostly flat and only slightly rocky beach. In these places, I would cast the nymph into the current, then jog alongside it, keeping pace with the stream, the whole while watching that little slice of orange for any sign that a trout was trifling with the fly.

Once, as I was running, I failed to see a branch and ran smack into it. Another time, I scared a fish that must have been sipping tiny insects off the surface. After these two incidents, I tried hard to keep a low silhouette. I ran hunched over like Groucho Marx. For the first time ever I started catching trout with a fly—on purpose.

* * *

The trouble was that the fish I was catching were mostly little ones, and I was catching them, almost exclusively, when the mayflies were hatching and the river was electric. At a time, that is, when it is a lot easier to take them. I realized from Dad's diary, and from his coterie of authors, that to be successful under less hospitable conditions I had to get the nymph down near the bottom of the stream, where trout apparently do most of their feeding.

There are several ways to do this. One is by adding weight. Following the recipe of Lee Wulff, I beaded the leader with tiny lead split-shot, so that it resembled a necklace, and hurled it into the flow. There are problems with this, I discovered. Much of the time, unless you fuss with the shot, the weight seems to retard the fly. You are never really certain that the nymph is drifting in sync with the current. Plus, using weight can be expensive: I kept catching the bottom and losing flies to the rocks.

There is also the difficulty of casting such a rig. You can't use your regular stroke, but pretty much have to lob the thing. Even then, you're likely to get it tangled up—or maim yourself, as I did one day when I let my back cast dip too low behind me. Coming forward with my usual stroke, I ripped the faded Yankees cap off the top of my head and routered a bloody groove in my scalp.

I was encouraged to look into the other ways of getting a nymph down—notably, by fishing upstream.

It seems like a small thing. All you're doing, after all, is turning around. But it changes everything.

For one, when you fish upstream, you don't have to worry quite as much about your approach to the water, an aspect of angling to which I initially paid little attention. For months, I would walk right up to the South Branch and start fishing, without giving any thought to whether the trout could see me.

This was almost okay when I was working the broken water, where the trout's window on the world above him is mostly blurred by the rushing current. It was not okay, though, when I was fishing the deeper pools where the trout's angle and clarity of vision is such that he can see you practically from the moment you park your car. It took me a while, too, to figure out that standing on top of boulders and casting was not all that smart either.

You do not have carte blanche when you fish upstream. You still have to think about your approach. But, as the trout generally faces into the flow, the upstream strategy permits you to take advantage of the blind spot directly behind him. It also enables you to sink your fly, to get it down into the thin layer of almost-still water along the bottom of the river where the trout tend to hold, especially at the beginning of the season when the water is high and cold and surly. ("It's April," Dad admonishes himself in the diary. "Fish up, dummy!")

Problems of drift and drag are reduced when you fish upstream, because the line is no longer—or, at least, not so much—the plaything of contending currents. This is because you are more or less casting into the same current you are standing in. Thus, the nymph can sink more quickly, especially if you add a dollop of weight to the leader.

This is the upside of upstream nymphing. The downside, I quickly saw, is that it can be a subtler game.

Fishing downstream, I found that the trout would sometimes hook themselves. They would take the artificial at the end of its drift, when it would begin to swing out below me and, at the same time, rise up through the water column, much as an emerging mayfly or caddis fly would do. If the trout struck at this point, I had a much better chance of feeling him because the line was taut.

Upstream nymphing is all about controlling slack. It's about putting slack into the line with your cast so the nymph will sink and drift back to you in a natural manner. Paradoxically, it's also about getting slack out of the line, so you can feel the take.

For weeks, months, years, on the South Branch of the Raritan, I found myself in the throes of a terrific guessing game. I would cast up into a pool or run, and I would strip the line from my rod as it drifted back toward me. I would watch that little orange flag for any hesitation, the slightest hint that a trout had taken the nymph into its mouth.

The trouble with nymphing is that you cannot tell, with any certainty, when the trout has waylaid your fly and begun its interview. By contrast, there is little doubt when a trout takes a dry fly, because it all happens on the surface in front of you. *You see the take*. But with the nymph, time after time I would lift the rod in response to some imagined strike, and I would find nothing on the other end.

I remember, as a little kid, making prank calls. My buddies and I would choose some name out of the phone book and dial the number, then hang up as soon as the party answered. Or, nastier still, we would sit on the line, listening as the party found increasingly colorful language with which to ventilate his anger. Over and over, we would do this. Pretty soon, the guy would stop picking up.

Often, nymphing upstream on the South Branch, I would stop picking up. Or, rather, I would pick up sometimes, but if I'd just had a run of prank calls, I would not answer the next few rings, even if the fly line stopped completely or took that telltale jog back upstream.

That's how spooked I would get.

I remember a conversation I had with Dad on one of the afternoons when we stopped for a couple of beers after fishing at his club. I remember asking him why he was so devoted to the lowly nymph. Why did he choose to dredge the bottom with these blobs of feather and fur that looked, well, like they just crawled out from under a rock, when he could be angling on top with some snazzy dry fly?

The question took my father by surprise. He had clearly never thought about it. "I don't know," he said. "When you start, you try all the flies— streamers, wets, nymphs, dries. And you come back to the ones that interest you."

I wish now that I had pursued the question. For I suspect that it goes to the heart of who my father was. But it wasn't the question that, after yet another hapless day on the trout stream, I was burning to ask. The next one was.

"The thing I still don't get with nymphs," I said, "is how do you know when there's a take?"

"You keep a tight line," my father said, "and you feel the fish down there, tapping."

"But what if you don't feel anything?"

"You watch the end of the line—or your leader, if you can see it. If the line jerks or stops, then you know."

"But couldn't it just be the bottom or a snag?"

"Yes," said my father, smiling. "It could."

"Is there any other way to tell?"

"Well, you could watch for a flash in the water."

"A flash in the water?"

"Yes, when a trout rolls to take a nymph, he will sometimes show his side or his belly."

"What if there is no flash?" I asked.

He put down his beer and thought a moment. He started to say something, then decided against it.

I don't know what was going through his mind. But if I had to guess, it would be this: some things in life can't really be explained. Like a belief in God or what love is or, maybe, how you catch a trout with a nymph.

"Good question," my father said.

Five

NICKY WAS A strange and wonderful little boy. For the first five years of his life, we lived in a huge four-bedroom co-op apartment on Manhattan's Upper West Side. No one we knew had such a place. We wouldn't have either, if Molly's mother had not sold a summer house and generously given us money needed for the down payment.

The living room had four tall windows with built-in seats. On weekend mornings, Nicky and I would sit in one and peer down at the traffic five flights below, as it percolated along Broadway. Taxis, buses, police cars, garbage trucks, street sweepers— or "sweep-keepers," as Nicky named them—would motor by, and we would call them out by turns, as if we were birders adding to our life-lists.

We would do this, seemingly for hours. Eventually, though, Nicky would get hungry, and he would let me know by launching into a nonsense rhyme we'd devised:

I'm thirsty as a cloud
And hungry as the moon.
I'm hungry as anything
I prezoon.

We would head off to the kitchen for breakfast.
But, first, Nicky would plant himself in front of the
living room clock, a figurine of a Yankee patriot with
a timepiece in its belly, and he would swing his head
like a pendulum until he got dizzy and collapsed in
a heap of laughter.

Nicky lived in an animistic universe, where
everything was potentially alive and fraught with its
own spirit. Each day Nicky and I would stand at the
mail chute in the hallway outside our apartment, and
we would watch as our letters, and sometimes letters
from the apartments above, would swoop and chatter
down the clear glass rectangle toward the lobby.
"Birds, Da Da!" Nicky would say, and he was right.
The letters looked like birds.

Nicky worked by analogy. His brain teemed
with nursery rhymes. In bed in the morning, I would
pull him onto my chest and see mischief in his eyes.
He would post up and down. Then, laughing, he'd
say, "Ride a cock horse to Banbury Cross, to see a fine
lady on . . . Da Da!"

Once, on my mother's terrace, he jumped in the
sandbox and banged his face. Ger took him in her
arms and rocked him, and he started to sing,
"Humpty Dumpty sat on a wall, Humpty Dumpty had
a great fall. . . ."

Nicky had a poet's gift for threading similarity

through difference. But the result was not always happy. Once my mother stayed overnight. She slept in my study, down the hall and across from Nicky's room. Up with the dawn, Ger wanted to use the bathroom, but the knob to the study came off in her hand. My mother was trapped. Yet she knew that we monitored Nicky through an intercom, and if she could get his attention, she could get ours too.

"Nicky," she called to him. "Door broken. Tell Da Da, door broken." He told us and my mother quickly got sprung.

For the next several weeks, though, Nicky was obsessed with doors. He was at pains to keep them open and gave a long, anxious look back every time a door closed behind him, or someone he loved. Then one day, his nanny went off to visit a friend.

"Fran is in Brooklyn," we told Nicky, and we watched his eyes grow large with fear.

"Fran broken?" he said, over and over.

There was no convincing Nicky that his Franny was all right, until late the next day when she miraculously re-appeared, smiling and in one piece.

Nicky had imaginary friends, a pair of mice named Shem and Dem and a rabbit named Carzell. Shem and Dem would "betect" him from evil. Nicky was afraid of things that didn't even begin to trouble other children. But he also had an extraordinary way of toying with his fears. I remember one bright fall afternoon hearing a shriek and running into the kitchen to find him standing by the window.

"Look, Da Da," he said. "I cut myself."

I looked. There was no visible cut on his arm.

"That looks bad," I said. "How'd you do it?"

"The sun did it," he said.

Nicky moved slightly and a diagonal of light slashed through the window and across his wrist.

"See," he said, cheerfully.

Nicky fell through the cracks of our divorce.

I didn't see it at the time. But that was the problem. Molly and I were too caught up in our own tragedies, too busy trying to plug the hole in our own lives to give proper attention to the one gaping in his.

Molly married again the day after our divorce came through. She married "a lawyer with the soul of a poet," or so he had billed himself in the magazine personals. Michael, from what I could see, was not a bad guy. He was just another lost soul trying to make a connection. No matter. Nicky had it in for him almost from the outset, not so much for who he was as for what he was: competition. My son was not willing to share his mother with another man, especially one who was not his father. And he was definitely not about to do this man's bidding.

Divorce brought Nicky and me together. It bound me to both of my kids in a way marriage never did. I'm one of those fathers, I suppose, who was given a second chance by divorce.

Before divorce, I was a privileged character, a self-styled artist in residence who made what amounted to appearances in his children's lives. I would come down from my third-floor garret and play with them, as if they were puppies. Then I'd disappear back into the creative ether.

Molly did most of the heavy lifting. She was the one who took the kids to the doctor's office, who shuttled them to friends' houses and music lessons, who helped them with their homework and dealt with their teachers.

Now, as a divorced dad, I had to do for them myself. For those couple of days and nights they were with me each week, I was a single parent. I had to learn to find my way around the A&P, iron Peter Pan collars as well as button-downs, cook something more nutritious than pancakes.

My kids were a godsend, an axe for the frozen sea inside me. But though I loved them equally, I didn't treat them the same.

Daughters, I think, are always easier for fathers. I don't know why. That just seems to be the way it is.

Sam was a blue-eyed, light brown-haired, six-year-old gumdrop. She was portable, adaptable, appropriate for all weathers. I took her everywhere I went—to the grocery, to my hockey games, bookstores, Home Depot. I just popped her in the Justy with the rest of my gear.

She was a tomboy who played games of catch with me, ice-skated and roller-bladed and swam with me. We went to endless movies together, from *101 Dalmatians* to *Ace Ventura Pet Detective*. Music was our glue. "Put on the rock 'n' roll," she would say the instant she got in the car, meaning anything by ZZ Top. We would dance together to Paul Simon's "You Can Call Me Al," and she'd go to sleep each night with the *Graceland* album as her lullaby.

Everything between us was grist for a routine. I

had to cut her food for her, in what she referred to as "that special way." Each night before she went to bed, we would read Lewis Carroll's "Jabberwocky" and engage in the same ritual exchange. "You're the best, big guy," I would say to her. And she would reply, "No, *you're* the best." Then, we would tell each other: "See you in the ayem."

I had a million nicknames for her. She was Slammin' Sammy Plummer, Sam "the Bam" Antha, the Preying Mantha, or just plain Manth.

I had dozens of names for my son, too. But it was different with Nick. With Nick, there was also work to do. I was busy trying to turn Nick into a man, a better man than I was.

At thirteen, Nicky was enjoying what appeared to be an *annus mirabilis*. He was, thanks to a growth spurt, a near-six-foot-tall junior high school hunk who made good grades and was a force in the local hockey league. One of his teachers called him the Golden Boy. This was the public Nicky, the one out there for popular consumption. But I saw him in the altogether. I saw the charlatan standing behind the wizard's curtain. I knew that Nicky was hanging by a thread.

His life was a study in chaos—not unlike his room, where the dustballs formed drifts in the corners and the clothes were a foot deep on the floor. Some of the clothes were dirty and some were clean, but there was no telling which was which. Rather than sort them, he cut a path from his bed to his computer, another from his bed to the door.

Typical teenage behavior? Maybe so, except that

his room was of a piece with everything else in his life. Nicky put everything off. He waited until the last minute to do his papers or study for tests, then stayed up all night and crammed for them. This was not so terrible in and of itself. Lots of people, myself for one, got through college this way. The trouble was, he'd be sick the next morning, especially if there were a test he feared taking. And if he weren't sick, he admitted in a moment of candor, he would sometimes stick a finger down his throat to induce vomiting.

Nicky's life was slowly whirling out of control. He could not contain his eating (a problem that was temporarily hidden by the growth spurt). He could not bring himself to exercise, to get in shape for hockey or lacrosse (although he claimed that he wanted to excel in each). He could not bring himself to ask teachers for recommendations, to call coaches to find out about games, to talk to people about sum-mer jobs. He was becoming increasingly reclusive. If left alone, he would sleep much of the day. . . .

"You've got to leave him alone," Ger would say to me, during telephone conversations that invariably concluded with one of us hanging up on the other. "You've got to realize that Nicky is not you."

"Who is he then?" I would ask.

"He is his own person. He's Nicky."

For years, I could not credit this idea. When I looked at Sam, I was able to see her. When I looked at Nick, my own flaws and frailties stared back at me. I felt doubly guilty about the kid: I not only deserted him, I gave him my toxic chemicals.

* * *

Nicky was caught between two worlds, childhood and adulthood. He had been cut adrift by divorce. His hostility to Michael, Molly's new husband, forced Molly to choose between them. And Molly, though she didn't mean to, chose Michael.

Sam did not force her mother to make this choice. She had little memory of Molly and me together. Molly and Michael, in fact, formed a tight new family around her.

It was a difficult fact for me to deal with, especially when she worked out the new complications in front of me. "I have two daddies," Sam would say to me. "You're my daddy, and Michael's my daddy too."

This sort of thing went through me like a knife.

Nicky, meanwhile, was anxious for me to love him. This was Nicky the child. But there was another Nicky. Nicky the would-be adult, who was determined to stand alone.

One minute, in my garage apartment which barely contained us all, the big lug would be rousting Sam from my lap and snuggling there himself, cooing "Da Da." The next minute he would be defying me on some matter that barely merits relating. But I'm going to relate one anyway. One Saturday, after fishing on the Amawalk, a small tailwater stream just north of Manhattan, I raced back to pick up Nicky and Sam. We were due at Ger's for dinner. I burst into Molly's kitchen and found Sam reading one of her favorite books about the Boxcar children. Nicky was heating up a chicken patty. I told him not to eat it, dinner was on the table in Clinton. We were already late.

Nicky said that he hadn't eaten anything since

morning and he was starving. I told him to eat an apple. That way he would still have an appetite.

He looked at me, bold face, and said, "No."

I could not believe that my son was disobeying me. He stood there, not challenging me exactly, but not budging either.

"What do you mean, 'No'?" I said. I could feel the blood surging up within me, spilling into my eyes.

"I mean 'No,'" he said. "Just 'No,' that's all."

I got out of there as fast as I could. I jumped in my car and drove to the end of the kids' street and just sat there. I cooled down, got hold of myself for once. I realized that all these people, my mother, my sisters, were waiting to see Nicky and Sam. It was not the time to play this out.

I walked back into the house and found Nicky on the cordless phone talking to Molly upstairs. He was telling her he was not going to his grandmother's. He was eating the chicken sandwich.

I told him that we were going, after all.

"Get your things and let's go," I said brusquely. "And throw away the rest of that sandwich."

No," he said. "I'm eating it. I'm hungry."

Somehow I left before I killed him.

I stayed away from him for a week. I wanted to give us each a chance to think about what had happened. Then, on a Monday night, while Sam was off learning soccer at Kinder Kickers, I swung by and picked up Nicky and took him to a local place with a reputation for its ice cream.

Nicky and I sat in the parking lot with our cones and talked, stiffly, about school and his birthday. Then I asked him about the other night. What did he think about it? He said he thought I'd been unfair. I tried to explain that, even if he thought I was wrong, he still had to obey me—that's what you did with your father. Nicky said he would obey me, but he wanted to have a say in what happened to him.

"You do have a say," I said. "You just don't have the last word. In many cases, I'm willing to compromise. Remember the other night, when you said you were starving, I said, 'Okay, eat an apple'?"

"This is not a democracy," said Nicky.

"You're right, it's not," I said.

We drove back in silence. But we resumed the argument in front of Molly's house, and I made it, as I often did, all or nothing. An apocalypse in a teacup.

I told Nicky that I couldn't have a relationship with him if he didn't obey me. I told him that I would have to back off, walk away from his life.

"Is that what you want?" I asked him.

"If that's the way you put it, yes," said Nicky.

I totally lost it. I didn't see that I had backed him into a corner. That I hadn't given him any choice. That I'd forced my son to stand up to me and answer me in equally final terms.

All I could see was that I was going to lose him, just as my own father had lost me. I was wild with frustration, blind with rage. I remember giving an animal cry of desperation, grabbing him and hitting him, actually pounding him with my fists in a pathetic attempt to beat him into tractability. It was dumb and brutish and I will never forgive myself for it, but I didn't know what else to do.

Nicky did not fight back, but covered his head with his arms, then burst from the car into the house. I could hear him screaming in outrage.

I remember the last time my father hit me. I was thirteen or fourteen, about Nicky's age. It happened in the bathroom of the little red house on the dead end street in Cranford where I grew up. I had said something unsavory that morning to Ger, after Dad left for work. It must have been especially bad, because my mother did not normally rat on me.

I was in the bathroom when my father came home. I heard him and my mother talking in the kitchen. Then I heard his voice rise in anger. "He said *what*? Where is he?"

Before I knew it, Dad was out in the hallway, saying he knew I was in there and ordering me to open the door. Then he was inside the tiny room, thrusting his face into mine.

There is something I have not mentioned about my father—the rage that burned within him with a low but steady flame. Where it came from, I honestly don't know. I suspect that it was in the bag of tricks he carried into the world.

I know that, on memorable occasions, he trained his anger on me. My father was only 5'9" and 170 lbs., but, to me, he always seemed much larger. On these occasions, his face would turn into a terrible mask of hatred, his fists would ball at his side, and his body would begin to shiver and all the air would be sucked out of the room.

I don't know how much of this was histrionic and how much was real. I do know that on this particular night my father hit me, as he had before. But this time was different. This time I hit him back.

We looked at each other in astonishment.

Then my father swung again, a roundhouse right that knocked me off my feet and into the bathtub. As I fell, I grabbed one of the shower knobs and ended up lying in the tub with water beating down on me.

We both started laughing. I don't know who laughed first, probably my father, as I must have looked ridiculous lying there in my sodden sweatshirt and chinos. It was the last time Dad ever hit me, and it was not that long after this that he began to pull back from my life.

Six

I'VE HAD TROUBLE sleeping all my life. It's a problem
that has been treated with varying degrees of sym-
pathy by my family and friends. I had one buddy,
growing up, who was especially attuned to my plight.
I remember one summer four of us ended up spending the night at another kid's place down on the Jersey
shore. Walter, this prince of a friend, made sure I got
the last bed. I bunked with our host, a kid I hardly
knew, while Walter and the others slept out on the
Boston whaler and put up with the swells that would
have had me puking all night.

In the days when every young single guy I knew
in Manhattan slept on a mattress on the floor, I slept
on one too. Only I kept another, smaller one in the
closet, in case a girl spent the night. I was so jealous
of my sleep that, when it came time to actually close
our eyes, I would talk the girl into removing to her
own berth. One friend, amused by the arrangement,
and my chutzpah, referred to the mattresses as the
"tug" pulled up beside the "liner."

This sleeping quirk was just one of several that made me seem, to my family, to be a workout. My sisters would routinely roll their eyes and whisper "good luck" to each girl I brought home.

Even at this point, I was still struggling to get more than four hours of sleep a night. I could not shut down my mind, especially after I managed to wreck things with Nicky.

I had learned long ago not to fight my insomnia, but to try to lie down in it. Sometimes I'd get up and watch television or read. Mostly, I'd settle back with my eyes closed and go to the theater of my mind, which on nights when my thoughts were user-friendly, I could pretty well program. I used to favor X-rated stuff, trysts with old girlfriends who had turned into sirens with the passage of time. But, increasingly, the late late show was given over to fishing.

I am unable to recall the names of people just met at a party or business lunch. I am bad about birthdays and anniversaries. I'm often incapable of remembering what story I wrote at *People* the week, or even day, before. But I can reconstruct the topography of a trout stream in my mind with a kind of fidelity that might interest the Army Corps of Engineers. I can recall the shape and rush and timbre of pools, detail each pillow and boil and funnel of moving water, each plunge and spill and cascade. And I can fish them as I lie in bed at night, my mind dancing along the foam line, swirling around each eddy, as, with any luck, I wend toward sleep.

I was besotted with fly-fishing. It was always there on the rim of my awareness, no matter where I was or what I was doing, angling for a way into conscious mind. People would be discussing the celebrated court case of the moment, and I'd hear them talking about "reasonable trout." Or the conversation might turn to the new Hopper exhibit and my mind would picture not some bleak city-scape where it's always three o'clock in the morning, but the winged insect that drives the fish nuts in summer. Or I would find myself cruising the cable channels late at night on my ancient twelve-inch Sony, and I'd realize I was looking for old Westerns on the chance that the Bighorn or the Rio Grande or the Missouri, famous fly-fishing rivers, would put in a cameo appearance. Or out driving with the kids on Sunday, we'd drop into a strange valley and I'd spot a couple of cars parked beside the road, and I would know in my bones that they were fishermen's cars and there had to be a trout stream through the trees.

For the most part, I am a responsible, fairly moral member of the race with a large capacity for guilt. Yet where fishing was concerned, I discovered that I was utterly rapacious, blindly and amorally opportunistic—a Snopes in Eddie Bauer clothing. I'd sneak off every chance I could. On weekends, I'd take Sam and head up to my mother's place in Clinton, stealing over to the South Branch at dawn. I would always plan to fish for just a couple of hours and be back before everyone awoke. Invariably, I'd stroll into the house around noon and discover a note saying they'd given up on me and gone to lunch. Or worse: I'd find my sister Kappy in the kitchen perched in a ladder-back chair, her eyes blazing disapproval.

During the week, it would take me an hour to get home from work, and another hour to get to the stream for that last, precious bit of fading light when the big fish start to move. If I didn't catch a story, I'd slip out after lunch on Wednesday, the day the magazine closed up tight, taking a calculated risk that I wouldn't be tapped for last-minute duty. I remember one day the office shut down early so everyone could attend a memorial service for an editor who'd been at *People* since the creation and who was revered for his ready wit. My own take: he was one of those guys who was tight with you when you were working together; otherwise, he passed you in the corridors with mute indifference. This was, admittedly, a self-serving analysis, but it allowed me to make for the stream without taxing my conscience.

I didn't tell anyone what I was doing. I didn't want anyone to know. It was somewhat like starting a book. It's disheartening to have to keep telling people that you're working on something. People mean well. They always ask, "How's the book going?" Maybe that day, or week, or month, it's not going at all. Or they ask, "What's your book about?" Maybe you don't know. Maybe you're just following a thread, hoping it will take you to daylight.

Most people knew that I was fishing, anyway. They thought it was "nice" that I was "carrying on the family tradition." But almost from the start my fishing was a more radical act than anybody, myself included, could have imagined.

I remember, around this time, reading a story in *The New York Times* about a woman from Nantucket with a magnificent garden. She had started it after her daughter died at twenty-nine. Only, at first, she wasn't really gardening; she was just digging, as a way to deal with her loss. "When I found that I couldn't do anything," the woman said, "I found that digging seemed to help. It was one of those things that you think of as being a mindless activity, but actually it was more than mindless. In fact, it was just the opposite, because my mind was doing the digging. . . . I never thought, 'Oh gosh, this digging is really good for me.' The garden got bigger and bigger, and one thing led to another. It took a while for me to realize that what I was really doing was trying to get rid of the grass, and that it should all be garden. Even then I never saw the big picture at any point."

My fishing, was like this wonderful lady's gardening, in that I turned to it when I found that I couldn't do anything else. It was different, though, because I was dimly conscious of why I was doing it: I knew that it was good for me (it beat moping around my apartment). But it would be some time before I would be able to see the bigger picture—that the real reason I was fishing, as Huey said in Montreal when she lit her candle, was to wish my father well.

Like every other rookie, I was drawn to the deep pools. The deeper the water, the more profound the spell it seemed to cast on me. There *is* something truly alluring about trout stream pools, something in their self-contained shape and near-narrative symmetry—each pool has a beginning, middle, and end—that strikes a primal chord in us.

Henry Thoreau compares a lake to the "earth's eye, looking into which the beholder measures his own nature." Similarly, the pool is the eye of the trout stream, a break in the marathon conversation between river and shore, a pause for reflection. A pool is a forest mirror, imaging back the trees and rocks that surround it, the sky above it, as well as the Narcissus who gazes down into it. It is also, famously, a holding pen for monster trout. In my mind I could see them arranged over the cobbled bottom like deep-bellied planes on a bombing run.

Whether the big fish were there or not, I can't really say. All I know is that I never seemed to catch them, although not for lack of trying. For months on end, I kept returning to the deep pools, hypnotically combing them with my nymphs.

Then, one day I had an experience that changed the way I looked at the South Branch. Late on a sunny afternoon, I was standing at the end of a deep slow pool, casting up toward the placid middle. I was actually in the riffles below the tail, with my rod tucked under my arm, foraging for something in one of the pockets of my vest. Suddenly, I felt the rod jump and was so startled I nearly dropped it.

I realized, when I collected myself, that a fish, and a pretty big fish at that, had whacked my fly as it passed through the water below me. I was amazed. I was standing in water that was less than a foot deep and that was busting across the rocks. I couldn't imagine that a trout could take up residence here, but clearly one had.

Looking behind me, just a dozen feet or so, I saw

a slightly darker patch in the general froth. It was about the size of a desktop. The water I saw was smooth on the surface. It was deeper too, I discovered, as I stepped in to my knees and sent the occupant that lived, or just fed, there speeding away.

It was in this manner that I was gradually weaned from the deep pools, that I learned to fish the riffles and glides of the South Branch, to look for windows in the tumult, places where the water grew a shade darker and slick on top, signaling that the bottom had dropped away, places sometimes scarcely bigger or deeper than a kitchen sink, where a twelve-inch trout could take shelter from the hurly-burly and still nose out to grab a meal.

I had already learned to pay special attention to runs, those places in the stream where the fast water loses some of its spunk and narrows and deepens into chutes and channels. A run is a sort of stunted pool, one that has been edited down; it's the body of a pool without the head or tail, the meat without the vegetables and potatoes.

The great thing about a run is that you can usually get right up on it. The water is busy enough that, if you take some care with your approach, the fish should not see you. In addition, the casting is often a less complicated matter because the currents in a run are easier to decipher. Often there will be one main current, snaking down the middle or along the bank, and it won't be hard to pick it out. Nature, no doubt with the tyro fly-fisher in mind, is inclined to mark it with a line of foam. The foam, in turn, collects bugs like flypaper. It also collects trout; they often park beneath it, awaiting the next plat du jour.

When a run is seriously interrupted by boulders, it's called pocketwater. The Gorge is maybe two miles long, and about one and one-half miles of that is glutted with rocks, some the size of a small pickup truck. The Gorge, in fact, is a pocketwater festival. But I was not initially one of the celebrants. I figured I already had enough chaos in my life. So I stayed away from the broken water and jockeyed with the other cowards for position on the pools and runs. Eventually, though, I was forced to fish it, especially on weekends, just to have a stretch to myself.

Pocketwater is fast, steep, shattered. The water bangs the rocks the way a numbered ivory ball does a billiard cushion. It even sounds louder than the rest of the stream. The footing is iffy and the wading treacherous; you are constantly battling the chop, stepping like a mountain goat from one risky perch to another. It also, in my experience, involves a certain amount of falling in the drink.

But I discovered that it's worth it because the trout are there and ready to be taken, as they get much less pressure than their peers in the pools and runs. The thing about pocketwater is: even if a stretch has been canvassed by a legion of slew-footed anglers, it is still a relative virgin; there will always be some cleft, some rent in the river's fabric that has not been thoroughly felt out.

Each pocketwater fish lives in his own myopic world. He has the rock he lives behind and a few feet of furry vision on either side of it. So there's no need to worry about spoiling the water with an errant cast.

On a pool or run, you make a bad pitch and that's it; the trout will quit feeding, sometimes for close to an hour. But in the pockets there's no ripple effect; the fish are oblivious to what's going on next door.

I found that pocketwater is actually great water to learn on because it's a mistake-free environment. It's not a place to work on long casts, but to develop your short game and confront the nasty business of drag. In the pools and runs, I would make long and, I thought, graceful pitches and assume that I was getting a drag-free float, when in fact the currents were tugging at the fly, creating, when I was fishing on top, a tiny "V" behind it that was imperceptible to me, but not to the trout, which made my lure for a phony. In pocketwater, there is no room for self-deception. The business of drag is brought out of the closet. The currents are so contentious that the fly will start to pull the second it hits the water.

The best way to deal with this, according to Ray Bergman, is to employ short casts, to clamber around on the rocks until you achieve a position from which to make a drag-free assault on the desired water. Sometimes, though, I just wasn't up to the drill. That's when I tended to experiment.

Fishing a bouldery stretch on the South Branch, I would find myself doing all sorts of weird things with the rod and line to give the fly a few precious seconds of hang-time in the fish's window before the currents had their way with it. I would come up with some strange new cast, which seemed to be evoked purely by the circumstances. Then I'd find out later, from one of Dad's authors, that it was not new at all, but some less efficient version of an already established cast. One day, for example, when I was hemmed in by trees, I looked behind me and spotted a patch of blue high up in the wall of green. So I turned partly around and daringly aimed my backcast there. This, I later learned from A. J. McClane, was a familiar arrow in every *Practical Fisherman*'s quiver, known as the "steeple" cast.

Another time I plopped a nymph on a patch of water behind a boulder and watched as a dark green head the size of my fist came up, the mouth hinging at precisely the moment the river chose to yank the fly away. Increasingly annoyed by this sort of interference, I worked up a sidearm heave that I would stop severely, causing the fly to swing around and drop in the water below the line—the idea being that the artificial would have an unhurried moment in the pocket before the line caught up and spirited it off. I was more than a little pleased with myself, until I read Swisher and Richards on putting candy cane shapes in your line with the "curve" cast.

Sometimes I'd make much this same fling, only overhand and with more oomph, sending the nymph knifing down through the water beside a rock. A similar maneuver called the "tuck," I later learned, was associated with Pennsylvania angler George Harvey.

But I had my own wrinkle. Now and then, when confronted with a deep juicy hole, I'd fire a weighted nymph at the rock itself, using it like a basketball backboard: the nymph would plunge straight to the bottom, even as the slack coiled on the surface. By the time the current tightened the line, the fish would have the fly in its mouth and, ideally, I'd feel him down there, tapping.

"Try to be one of those people on whom nothing is lost," says Henry James to the young novelist. It is good advice, I think, for the novice fly fisher. I know that I was trying to be one of those people. I was learning by accident, through indirection finding direction out. Never mind that I was simply going where many others had been, redoing what had already been done many times before.

It was through another fluke that I found my way back to the trout stream pools. One warm September day, after doing nothing for hours in the Gorge, I sat down on the bank across from a deep trough that ran about fifty feet along the base of a sheer wall of rock. The moment my butt met the ground I was overcome with exhaustion. Before I leaned back and closed my eyes, I pitched a big nymph into the sluggish center of the trough.

Half an hour later, I got to my feet and picked the rod up off the ground—the tip was actually in the water—and suddenly felt a fish on the line. I was more than surprised; I was shocked. I felt the way I did when Nicky used to hide behind his bedroom door and jump out at me.

Later, I realized what I'd done. When I picked the rod up, I caused the artificial to lift off the bottom, much as a real nymph does when it begins its climb to the surface. I realized, too, after I'd taken two more trout much the same way over the next few days— only this time on purpose—that I had a method for fishing the pools, for working the still water where you couldn't depend on the flow to animate your fly. I also realized that I had read about the tactic in Bergman; in fact, I'd seen it put into action.

That's what Dad was doing those times at his angling club, when he stood at the end of the Stony Brook pool and cast into the sluggish middle. I remembered him standing there, waist-deep in the flood, nothing moving but his left hand, which fingered back the flesh-colored line with an impossibly slow retrieve. Sometimes when I looked up from my spot at the head of the pool, Dad would not be moving at all. Even his left hand would have gone quiet. My father would be standing there, letting his nymph settle on the bottom, grave and still as a heron.

I had grown up thinking of my father as a loser on land and as a magician on water. It was an easy formulation, but I never really questioned it.

The first part of the equation was dictated by my eyes; the second by that stunted organ, my heart. In some part of my misguided being, I must have felt guilty about thinking so little of my father when I was young. Thus I was always willing, even eager, to grant him prowess as a fisherman. And then I started to read his diary, to read it closely, marking it for use and emulation, and I discovered it to be riddled with passages of frustration and ineptitude.

"Got to club at 5:45 P.M.," he writes in June 1982. "Nothing doing till 8. Heavy sulphur hatch in Home Pool but couldn't get a strike & big fish coming up all around." A few days later, he writes again of "fish coming up. But still couldn't match the hatch.

Hooked nymph in my angling net & quit at 7:30."
And a few days after that: "Fish hitting short.
Nothing doing in 3 weeks. Why?"

I didn't know what to do with this picture of him.
I didn't want to believe that Dad was just another bum-
bler on the trout stream. Besides, it didn't square
with the things I'd heard about him, especially from
the younger men I'd met from his fishing club who
clearly idolized him. (There was something else, of
course. I had not yet learned about "the long
silences," as Thomas McGuane calls them, the unpro-
ductive periods of fishing. I was naive enough to
think that expert anglers caught fish all the time,
merely by virtue of their being expert.)

Then, one day, while reading the vexing sec-
tions of the diary, I realized something new and, for
me, revolutionary about my father: he was not interested in his successes, which he noted in passing, but
just in his failures. Only I don't think that he considered them failures. He considered them hard nuts to
crack, tough questions still to answer. I realized that
my father was like most other men I know. He was
interested in problems—in solving them, to be sure,
but mostly in just having them to wrestle with.

I used to regard my father as someone who did
not want to think. I used to believe that that was why
he turned to restoring antiques: he could go up to his
barn and bury himself in the donkey work, the endless sanding; he chose it, I felt, because he didn't
have to use his mind.

On an autumn day a few years after my father's
death, I went fishing in the Gorge with one of his

friends, a physician who sidelines in psychotherapy and whom Dad had gone to see when he was at his nadir. During a break, we pulled out folding chairs and sat in the sun, and Watty John regaled me with stories about meeting Einstein and palling around with Bob McNamara, years before he joined John F. Kennedy's cabinet. Somewhere in the conversation, I confided in Watty that I used to believe Dad had taken up his line of work because it enabled him to dodge his mind. Surprised, and clearly irritated by this admission, Watty responded, "What made you believe your dad wasn't thinking while he was up in his barn? I'd guess that was the charm of his work, the chance it gave him to think."

The world did not requite my father (at least, not while I was growing up and he and I were forging our relationship). The things my father did well the world did not seem to notice or value. As I've gotten older, I have seen this happen to a number of men— to bright, energetic people with genuine curiosity and original minds. You know them when they are young and full of promise. The years pass, you lose track of them; then you meet them again and you learn that they are delivering the mail, or selling clothes at the men's store you went to as a kid, or maybe substitute teaching at the local high school.

I used to wonder why these men, with their shining minds, were just scraping by, when so many lesser beings were making huge salaries and/or seeing their names in lights. The conventional notion is that they have no drive. But I no longer buy that (perhaps, because I realize that I am more like my father than I once could have imagined). I think now that these men have plenty of drive, just nowhere they can stomach driving to.

I used to think that my father retreated from the world. I still think that, but now I believe that his was a strategic—and, in many ways, admirable—retreat. I am reminded of Hemingway's *In Our Time*, an early collection of stories spliced together with vignettes, many of them about World War I. In one vignette, a wounded Nick Adams (after whom I named my own boy) is propped up against the side of a church in an Italian town. He spots Rinaldi, a more grievously injured soldier, lying face down by a wall. "You and me," he yells to Rinaldi's near-lifeless form, "we've made a separate peace."

That's what Dad did. He quietly declared his own separate peace. He turned his back on the world of getting and spending, of failing and succeeding— the world my mother and most other people I know claw to get ahead in, the world I was primed to enter—and he fixed his gaze on restoring antique furniture and fly-fishing.

I'll never know what engaged my father about working with old wood and veneers. He left no guide, no map. I do know that fly-fishing offered him a constant stream of problems worth his sinking his teeth into. For I have his diary.

The problem for me, though, was piercing the surface notation of the diary to discover what exactly is turning my father on, or off, in any given entry. And yet sometimes what's eating him is almost comically clear. "Your leader is sinking & it has to stay afloat in the fast water or you can't strike quickly," he writes at one point. "*So grease it.*"

The diary is shot through with this sort of thing, self-administered knuckle-rappings that I might have stitched into samplers and hung in the closet where I kept my gear. "You are not alert on first cast into any area." Amen. "You need to adjust your leader for different water." Right on. "You're leaving too soon. They probably start rising at dusk." Ditto. "You are forgetting terrestrials."

Huh? Forgetting *terrestrials*? I didn't know what terrestrials were until I read this entry, which, in turn, led me on a chase along Dad's bookshelf, until I lit upon Vince Marinaro's *A Modern Dry-Fly Code.* There I found chapters on the Japanese beetle, the grasshopper, and other insects that do not hatch in the water, but land on it, often with help from a sudden gust of wind, and that make up a substantial part of the trout's diet in the dog days of summer.

Trout are crazy about terrestrials. I remember the first time I put on a Jay-Dave Hopper. It was a sultry August afternoon and I was fishing the Pequest where it twists through a meadow. After coming up empty with nymphs, I threw the hopper pattern onto a narrow, bank-hugging run and watched two big rainbows, like red-striped silver commuter trains switched onto the same track, come roaring from either end and actually crash into each other. When the smoke cleared, alas, I had neither.

And then there was the business of night fishing. I knew that people lingered on the stream past dark. But I had no idea that they did it on purpose, until I came upon an entry in which Dad talks about forgetting to bring his fishing light to the stream, and another in which he inveighs against the "damn thing" for not working.

The very evening I read these entries—or, better, truly trained down on them, for I must have read them numerous times before—I reported to the Gorge equipped with my trusty Home Depot flashlight. When I got there it was about nine and already dark, and I had to wedge the flashlight in a tree to tie on the wooly bugger. It was midsummer, and the water had been like bathwater during the day. The fish had been off their feed all week.

Or so I thought. I learned differently on the third or fourth cast, when I pitched the streamer upstream and mended the line as it passed below me. I felt the bugger begin its tour through the tail of the pool and, then, a terrific jolt, as what had to be a huge trout tore into it. I not only lost the fly and the fish, but also the flashlight when, in a mad attempt to grab my line, I hurled it into the night.

Tingling all over, I raced up the embankment to my car and opened the door in order to have sufficient light to tie on another streamer. Then I crashed back down to the water, where several casts later I was fast to another good fish. The trouble was, I couldn't see to get him off the hook, so I had to trudge back up the embankment, dig the keys from my blue-jeans pocket, and open the car door again—this while a fifteen-inch trout slimed the front of my shirt. Twice more I did this, until the adrenal rush subsided and I was able to call it a night.

This is the way it went for me with Dad's diary: the lessons were paid out precisely when I needed them, when I was ready to take them in and put them to use. Somewhere in the back of my mind, for instance, I'd be wondering if there were more to nymphing than fishing the artificial across and down and swinging it like a wet fly, or casting up and dead-drifting it back to me. Then I'd come across an entry like this one on July 13, 1983: "Got to club 5:15. Water low, clear, temp 65. Fished Club Pool with dark dry #16. Hooked 6, released all. Went to Wright's [pool], got into dozen more. Didn't do a thing with Isonychia. Your mistake with Isonychia nymph is no action."

The idea of putting "action" on the nymph opened yet another window for me—this one onto the history of fly-fishing itself. It took me back to the early part of the century and the virtual invention of nymphing by G. E. M. Skues, who wrote about it in *Minor Tactics of the Chalk Stream* and caused a major row in British angling circles. Nymphing, I discovered, was greeted as an arriviste, as a low and unchivalrous form of deceit, by most English gentlemen who angled religiously with the dry fly.

In retrospect, Skues's heresy was mild compared to that of the next infidel, Avon riverkeeper Frank Sawyer. Where Skues had the decency to fish his flies on or near the surface, Sawyer had the gall to weight his nymphs (he tied his pheasant tail nymph with copper wire) and to fish them from the bottom up, wherever the trout were dining.

Not satisfied with adding weight, Sawyer put action on his nymph with a maneuver that came to be known as the "induced take." It's a simple but delicate matter of raising the tip of the rod when the nymph is a foot or two in front of the feeding trout. The idea is that a great deal of stuff, some of it food, some not, is passing before the trout's eyes and there is a better chance of getting him to choose your offering if it moves in a manner that suggests life.

Sawyer, though, was operating on the gin-clear English chalk stream, where the trained eye can make out a fish forty or fifty feet away. Sawyer could see where his fly was in relation to the trout he wanted and perform his lift at the opportune moment. He would frequently see the take itself, what old Skues called the "little white blink" of the trout's mouth as it opened to engulf a nymph.

On the South Branch, I'd seldom see the fish, much less the take, except when they were rising. Compared to Sawyer's Avon, the water on this largely rain-fed stream is fast and murky, and the trout generally take up lies that offer them concealment from predators, as well as access to the cafeteria line. This is to say that most of the time on the South Branch, I would not be casting to a particular fish, but to a particularly fishy-looking spot. Of necessity, I had to learn to read the water.

Reading the water. Maybe it's the old academic in me, but I love that phrase. I love the notion that a stream is a text, a system of signs that must be deciphered; that, like a good book, a trout stream gives up more of its meaning each time you come back to it; that it teaches you how to read other streams.

I came to see that trout are in love with the edges

of things, that they are shady, seamy characters who work the fringe. Trout like places where fast meets slow, where deep gives in to shallow. You could follow the foam line, and the feeding trout would probably not be far away. You could look for obstructions, for rocks and logs and shelves. For banks, both undercut and overhung. For bends in the river and eddies, where the gently whirling water presents the day's buffet as if on a lazy Susan.

So much of nymphing takes place in the mind, especially on a stream like the South Branch. I would cast my fly along the edge of the faster water at the top of a pool or run and I would chart its journey in my head. I would picture the nymph churning in the froth, then tumbling down into the deeper element, down, down, down, then ticking slowly across the rocks on its way back toward me.

I would envision the trout holding in the stillness at the end of a log, say, or beneath the lip of a cascade. He would be watching the nymph and he would be wondering if it were food and if he should take it in and find out.

At just that projected moment, even as I imagined the trout turning for a last, quizzing look before the nymph washed forever downstream, I would perform riverkeeper Frank Sawyer's storied maneuver. Slowly, steadily, I would lift the fly rod and wait to feel the throb of life on the other end.

Seven

THE RIVER WAS becoming a kind of sanctuary for me. On the South Branch of the Raritan, I was not a writer who was not writing. I was not a divorced man who was incapable of having a relationship with a woman. Above all, I was not a father who was finding it difficult to raise his kids.

Things were still tense with Nicky. But they were also, I thought, getting better. For a time, after I mugged him in the car, he wouldn't take my calls. Then we went through a period where he took the calls but answered me in monosyllables. He was understandably intent on punishing me. Now, some months later, he was still reluctant to come over to the apartment with Sam. But he was beginning to volunteer the details of his life over the phone.

More than anything I had wanted to build a sturdy bridge to my son before adolescence set in. But I was afraid that instead I had merely deepened the moat around him. I was afraid I was going to lose

Nicky, and not just for the next few years, but completely, the way Dad lost me.

Molly and Michael had bought a house together and ceded the third floor to Nick. The kid had his own ample bedroom stamped with his own inimitable decor (one poster was "Penises of the Animal Kingdom"). He had his own bathroom, his own phone line, his own computer, his own color TV. He had a girlfriend, a wafer-thin blonde who thought the sun rose and set on his shoulders, and a brace of male friends who were also under his spell.

Nicky had created his own little world. I could not help feeling that he had built this stronghold both because his mother and I had let him down and to preclude the possibility of our letting him down again.

He had everything he needed. He certainly did not need an inconsistent and intrusive father who one moment was currying his favor (I bought him the phone and TV) and the next was attempting to put him through boot camp. I would call Nicky up and say, "Why don't you come over for dinner?"

"You mean dinner and a lecture," he'd respond.

I couldn't really argue with him.

Finally, he did come over with Sam, and he spent the night. I was dealing with a wicked cold, and Nicky was unusually considerate, doing the dishes without being asked. He clearly wanted things to be better between us. We both did. But the next day we regressed to previous form.

In that tiny apartment with no doors, except the

one for the bathroom, Nicky managed to sleep until noon. I fixed him breakfast and suggested he help me out by vacuuming. He looked as if I'd asked him to pour molasses into his computer. I told him what he already knew: that I was not well, that it took all my energy just to stay vertical.

I busied myself in the kitchen, making lunch for Sam, who entertained me by reading out loud from one of her favorite books, *The Last Basselope*. I made the mistake of looking over to see how Nicky was doing.

He was randomly pushing the vacuum, missing whole areas of the rug and floor. I just stood there at the kitchen counter, buttering Sam's bagel and seething, knowing that I was being screwed with. Finally, I went over and took the machine from his hands.

"Look," I said, trying to stay cool, "you have got to have a plan. You've got to set up a grid in your mind and do it sector by sector. Otherwise, you don't know what you've done and what you haven't. See?"

I gave the machine back to him, but he wouldn't take it. "I'll never do it the way you want," he said. "Why don't you just do it yourself?"

"All right," I said. "I will."

I took him home. He said that he had made arrangements with friends to go bowling or to the mall or something. But a few hours later, when I brought Sam back, I found him in the living room playing a video game. He had obviously just wanted to get away from me. I didn't say anything.

Later that night, we got into it again. Three years after my banishment from the local youth ice hockey league, I had been asked to coach again. I declined the invitation to run my own team and decided instead to assist a friend, who counted Nicky as one of his best skaters.

We were sitting in the car in the parking lot by the rink. It was a Saturday night, as I recall, and I told Nicky that we were expected the next day at my mother's. We were going to help her clean out her attic or transport furniture to a show house she was decorating. I don't remember exactly what the task was. What I do remember is Nicky saying he couldn't do it.

"Why?" I asked.

"I've got plans," he said.

"Really? Who with?"

"My friends."

"Just like you did today, right?"

"I made a mistake. The plans were for tomorrow."

"Well, you'll have to cancel them."

"I can't."

"Why can't you?"

"Because we made them weeks ago."

"Look, I'm sorry, but you'll just have to tell your friends to go ahead without you."

"Why should I?"

"Because your grandmother needs you."

For me, that was the clincher; there should be no further argument. But I could tell that he remained unconvinced. At the risk of serving up another lecture, I proceeded to tell him that it didn't matter if he had plans with his friends. Friends, no matter how close, are ships passing in the night. Family comes first, especially if it's your grandmother, with no man to help her.

WILLIAM PLUMMER

"I don't feel the way you do about family,"
he told me.

"Really," I said. "How do you feel?"

"I feel like my friends are my family."

We sat quietly for a moment. I felt like I didn't
know who Nicky was, like I was sitting next to a
stranger. I didn't feel angry at him. In a way, I think,
I felt sorry for him.

I found myself on that precipice again. Things,
as always between Nicky and me, were tending
toward finality. Only this time I was not angry, but
sad, defeated.

Looking back, I'm not sure whether it was a last,
calculated attempt to force him out of his protective
shell, to force him to acknowledge me, his flawed
father, and the rest of the people who loved him. Or
whether I was just too weary of wrangling, too beaten
down, to get out of the car. But I told my son that if
he felt no obligation to his grandmother, then I felt
none toward him. I told him I was not going to skate
with him that night or any other night. So he could go
on into the arena by himself. He obviously didn't
need me any more. Maybe he never did.

Nicky surprised me. I figured he didn't give a shit
if I was at that practice or not. But he did. He apparently felt the pain of the growing rift between us as
sharply as I did. Or rather, as I had, because, at that very
moment, I was too drained to really care.

"Dad, you *have* to come in with me," he said,
crying. "You can't leave me. You're all I've got!"

Eight

BEFORE I STARTED fishing, I never paid much attention to the change in season, except of course as it had to do with sports. When I was a kid, sports were my life. They were the place where my father and I got together. I played football in the fall, ice hockey in the winter, baseball and tennis in the spring and summer; and Dad was always right there with me, with a glove or racket, stick or ball.

We played hockey on the frozen Rahway River, games of shinny with cages slapped together out of discarded boards and chicken wire. My father and his cousins and old high school classmates would have us out there after the first serious spell of cold weather, skating on black ice just a couple of inches thick. Often the cops would ask us to get off. This was when our parents were present. When they weren't, the cops would *order* us off, sometimes chasing us. My buddies and I would skate with our sneakers dangling from our belts, so they couldn't take our shoes.

Later, when I was in high school, Dad refereed

many of my games, invariably played on outdoor rinks at 6 A.M. in temperatures so cold you couldn't feel your toes. But it was in baseball that our relationship reached its apogee.

On summer nights, my father would rush home from work in New York, and later from Newark, to hit grounders to me with a rubber-coated hardball on the unpaved dead end street in front of our house. My buddies and I would see him coming from the top of the street, taking off his jacket, loosening his tie, starting to unbutton his shirt like Clark Kent, as he hurried past us and into the house. By the time he reappeared in a fraying polo shirt and paint-spattered khakis, my friends would be gone, safely tucked away in their houses, wanting no part of Dad's nightly baseball training camp.

Years later, while I was in graduate school and beginning to reach some preliminary understanding of my father, I captured this scene in a poem, which my mother framed and hung for a time in our kitchen. It was an unusual poem for the me I was back then—without a trace of irony.

DAD

> I want you to know that
> when you used to hit
> rubber-coated hardballs
> (that bounced two short
> then one long) on dead-end
> gravel-slick Bargos Place and
> Lefty and Ricky A. and the Chase boys

and whoever else had been playing
before you came fled
in mortal terror and I stayed
to field those vulcanized darts
with my ribs, my clavicle, my lower lip,
my guts in the dusk
for dread of the loss of Heaven
(the pain of Hell) in your eyes,
I never doubted your love.
I knew that each grounder,
each line drive, each popped-up mistake
bespoke feeling words despaired of.
I knew why you screamed
those rubber-coated BBs at me
and why when you picked up
your mitt after hitting I reared back
to EastJesus to make your hand smart.
We were saying: "This is for all you are
and will always be.
This is for all you'll never be.
And by God you are going to feel it
and you are going to know
it's I who say it and
will never stop saying it
even though they pave over
and make through our dead-end street
even though they stop making
rubber-coated hardballs." Dad.

Like every other kid growing up in America, I read
endless poems about spring. The anthologies we used
in grade school were filled with them. So were the

texts we read in college and that I taught from later on while plodding after a Ph.D. in English—verse ranging from eighteenth-century British poet James Thomson's dreamy invocation, "Come, gentle Spring! ethereal mildness come," to e. e. cummings' celebration of a time of year "when the world is mud-luscious" and "puddle-wonderful" and Henry Reed's naughty "Naming of Parts": "The early bees are assaulting and fumbling the flowers: / They call it easing the Spring." I read these poems, and taught them, purely as verbal contraptions—in part because that's what I was trained to do; in other part because I never understood what all the fuss was about spring. I didn't get the poet's rapture because I lived apart from nature, because the climate I inhabited was regulated, not by the sun and the rotation of the earth, but by the kitchen thermostat.

Fishing changed that, especially when after four years of waiting I was admitted to Dad's club.

The club is maybe ten miles upstream from the Gorge, but it seemed to be situated on a different river. The South Branch roars through the Gorge. It slows and fans out into the occasional pool but, for the most part, it presents the dynamic, boulder-strewn aspect of a western stream. The river above Long Valley clips along at a gentler pace. There are long flats marked by grooves and basins where the current has troweled out the bottom; riffles that become glides that turn into miniature pools; plunge pools created by amateur trout stream engineers; long, irregular runs winding past thickly fringed and severely undercut banks; and actual holes, deep, dark, mysterious places where, for no clear reason, the river tilts and all the water goes.

The upper portion of the South Branch has the character of a woodland stream. It is smaller, colder, purer water. Where the Gorge is cobbled with rocks, the floor of the angling club water tends to be sand and gravel. The South Branch flows from a natural lake, but it is also, in its upper section, fed by a limestone acquifer.

When you descend to the club's lower venue, you enter a different, wilder world. I don't want to suggest that you walk into the wilderness, or even into a full-fledged forest. Even when you are at the bottom of the club's mile and a half or so of water, you can hear the sound of trucks in the distance, busting along Route 513 toward Chester. No matter. Henry Thoreau could see train smoke from his cabin at Walden Pond. It did not take away his feeling that he was firmly in the woods.

There is a notion, peculiar to people who write about the outdoors, that nature is shy, elusive, secretive. It goes all the way back to the Greeks. "Nature is wont to hide herself," says Heraclitus. I'm sure he's right, although when I first went into the woods, I wasn't looking for nature (much less Nature). My gaze was fixed on the water and catching trout. The rest was window dressing.

The problem was, I think, that my angling life was still tangled up with my life away from the stream. There were days when I would arrive at the South Branch in a funk and thought to use fishing the way I'd always used exercise. Much as I would go to the gym and ride the stationary bike to near exhaustion, I'd drive to the river determined to fish it hard, thinking if I could pound up some trout, I might be able to change the weather in my head.

There was something else. I'm one of those people, I'm sorry to say, who is forever measuring his life. So it was inevitable that I would gauge my success as a fly fisher, and as a man—for fishing was the serious thing I was doing with my life—by how many trout I caught. On fishless or near-fishless days, I'd feel this dark wave come over me. I'd fight it, when I could, knowing only too well that this was the kind of thinking—this habit of seeing everything in terms of outcome, of reducing an enterprise of the spirit to material terms—that was leeching the joy from my life.

Then something happened. I'm not sure what or when exactly, although it was not that long after I joined Dad's club. I began to come to the stream in a different head. I stopped, or at least I tried to stop, using the South Branch as a proving ground or therapeutic spa. I made an effort not to carry my "taint" into the woods, as Faulkner calls it in *The Bear*, but to leave my woes in the club parking lot. Sometimes I would sit in my car until I felt I was in the right mind to approach the stream (until my posture was closer to that of supplicant than mendicant; my hand open, not out). And I was rewarded, I think, not with trout—although I did seem to take more fish when I wasn't trying so hard— but with an awakening to the natural world.

I received word of my admission to the club just before Christmas, and that day, or the day after, I jumped into my Ford Explorer—my mother had finally convinced me to retire the Justy—and drove to the South Branch. The temperature was below freezing, but I didn't notice or really care. It didn't faze me either, a week later, when I tripped entering the stream and took an impromptu bath. I remember that I continued to fish for several hours, until my shivering turned into outright palsy and I could no longer make a decent cast. That winter I fished at least twice a week, making certain to be on the water if the air temperature even thought about climbing past fifty. So I was there, in the woods, when the wildflowers arrived.

I saw the skunk cabbage first, with its speckled, coiled leaves screwing up through the partially frozen earth like a wine bottle opener through a cork. And the pussy willows, with their silver-white flowers that shed black bud scales on your clothes as you brushed by them on your way to the water. Soon, as March tipped over into April, the little woods began to hum with flowers—with white-blossomed bloodroot, porcelain-colored spring beauties, dogtooth violets and bluebells—making their rush to daylight before the trees filled with leaves and blocked the sun.

I began to carry a guide to wildflowers inside my fishing vest, getting off on the names (jack-in-the-pulpit, Dutchman's breeches, butter and eggs, and so on) and the weirdnesses (each year the bloodroot eats the hind end of its root and adds a new section to the front, in an all-consuming effort to renew its root stock), the festive colors (red, yellow, white, orange, brown, pink, blue) and funky shapes (tubes, bells, spikes, stars, funnels, pipes). I felt a little like Adam turned loose in the Garden, and I couldn't help noticing what I took to be patterns. By May, the buttercups were staking out the club parking lot and the marsh marigolds, with their heart-shaped leaves, were installed at streamside. Was there a color sequence? Was May the month for yellow flowers? Probably not. By May, the dandelion-like colt's foot was already afoot and the black-eyed Susans and golden-rod waited just down the road.

I did not have so fine or educated an eye that I could always tell the difference between Queen Anne's lace and, say, cow parsnip, or even periwinkles and blue-eyed grass, assorted asters and flea-bane. But I knew enough to be of two minds about the purple loosestrife, an aggressive invader that rubs out more fragile species; to exchange salutes with the day lillies, which line the highway like casino greeters; and to peer into the dull pink pom-poms of the joe-pye weed, which serve as a twenty-four hour convenience store for all kinds of insects: butterflies and bees by day, moths at night, with spiders always lurking, like crocs at an African watering hole.

And then there were the birds. By late February, the sparrows, cardinals, and finches would begin to work out their lungs. Then the red-winged males would arrive and drown out the winter songsters with their endless bickering over streamside real estate. I remember one afternoon sitting in the club parking lot and hearing a commotion across the road. Getting out of the car and walking over, I saw a huge flock of blackbirds in the farmer's field. They were red-wings or starlings or grackles, I couldn't tell what for sure, and they were in the trees at the far end, about two hundred yards away. There were hundreds and hundreds of birds, and every time I walked toward them they would take to the air, bundle briefly, and recede to the next layer of trees. It was eerie. I felt as though I were in the middle of a trick painting or some interactive computer game.

I had always thought of robins as suburban birds. But I quickly discovered that they are not just in the well-tended borough parks and backyards, but in the orchards and open fields as well. Robins are actually woodland birds. I would see them in the forest clearings with their bright yellow bills tugging earthworms from the soil, the worms resisting, digging their stiff, leg-like bristles into the ground. And anyone who fishes knows the belted kingfisher, the clown prince of the trout stream. With his oversized beak, bad '50s haircut, and thick white collar, he looks like he was whacked together on a bet. Most birds try to blend with their surroundings. Not the kingfisher, a nervy fellow who screeches up and down the stream. Once I watched one, high in a tree, bang a bait fish to death on a branch before consuming it in a single, elongated gulp.

Nature is red in tooth and claw. I know this, of course, and I know that it is uncool to anthropomorphize. But I can't help feeling that nature has her tender side as well. I am thinking of a midsummer bird that arrives at the South Branch just after the warblers pass through. The cedar waxwing is the kingfisher's aesthetic foil: where the kingfisher seems to have been forged from mismatched spare parts, the waxwing is clearly an original, a sleek and whimsical instance of nature's art. The waxwing is drawn in muted colors, its soft, seemingly air-brushed plumage a blend of delicate browns and grays with pale yellow; its wings are tipped with red. The mischief is in the bandit's mask, edged with ivory, which covers its eyes.

Cedar waxwings are devoted parents, likely to buzz any fisherman who ventures too close to the nest. They are devoted to each other, too, I think. They time their arrival at the South Branch to coincide with the ripening of the berries. One bright morning, using the binoculars I often carry, I watched a pair go through their courting ritual: one of the birds, the male presumably, eased up next to his mate, rubbed himself against her breast, ran his bill along her bill, then hopped back to his place on the branch. She proceeded to dance to where he was and requite the gesture. Then she hopped back to her spot. They went on this way for several minutes, until the male abruptly flew off, only to return with a shiny red berry in his beak, which, wings shaking, he skipped over and gave to her.

I found that, focusing on the water in that intense, thorough-going way that fly fishers do, nature leaked in from the periphery. When my mind was right, I didn't have to scout out, or even consciously look for, the creatures that lived in the woods. I had only to go about the business of trying to catch trout, and the residents would each, as Henry Thoreau suggests, step up and exhibit themselves.

I remember one day stalking a rising trout, slipping down along the bank to the bottom of a run, while trying to keep a low silhouette and never losing sight of the spot where the fish was coming up. At the bottom, I started to step back into the stream, when I felt something pull at the corner of my eye. It took me a moment or two to properly make it out. Holding a few yards above me was a snapping turtle. Maybe three feet across the back, he wafted in the mild bankside current like an underwater kite.

Another time, I was tucked in a cleft in an alder scrim along the Moon Pool. I was tying a new tippet to my leader when I heard a splash, then another splash, and another and another. A family of otters had landed.

They swam up and down the pool, sometimes on their backs, sometimes on their stomaches; sometimes their entire bodies were visible, other times just their heads. One otter, probably the mother, was clearly bigger than the others. At one point, they all floated past me on their backs. They looked like a synchronized swim team, their long ears tight against their heads, as if they were wearing bathing caps, paddling smoothly beneath the surface with their webbed paws. As if on signal, they all dove at once.

The otters appeared to be playing, but I don't think they were. I suspect that the mother was teaching the kids to fish, because a minute or so later they rose *en famille* to the surface, and one of the young otters had what looked to be a tiny brookie trapped between his paws. He swam on his back, as best he could, to the bank thirty feet above me, with the other two youngsters in hot pursuit. I couldn't see what happened next. But the precocious pup must have been mugged by his siblings, for a major row ensued.

Most of my exchanges with the inhabitants of the woods seemed to take place on the fisherman's path, which was probably first blazed by the animals themselves. I was forever running into Canada geese. In the early spring, it was no problem. I would hear them gabbling and honking; then they would see me and make tracks in the other direction. The difficulties started, long about April or May, when they had their young and were reluctant to surrender the right of way. Once I called the bluff of a gander who was hissing and puffing himself up in front of me, swinging his head and neck like a cobra. There were briers on either side of the trail and I didn't much feel like fighting my way through them. Besides, I was sure the gander was all show. He wasn't. The enraged bird came flying at me, and I ended up in the briers anyway.

There were other, more numinous encounters, notably with deer. Deer get bad press these days, especially in the northeast. There are upwards of 150,000 in New Jersey alone, where they are no longer regarded as the noble whitetail or Bambi, but as vermin with hooves.

Deer browse in suburban yards, ruin flower beds, devour farmers' crops. They bound across highway barriers and get smacked by cars. If you drive early enough into the rural areas, you see their carcasses beside the road. They lie there stiff and bloated, their feet weirdly kicked up into the air. Add to this the fact that deer carry the tick that causes Lyme disease, and it is no wonder property owners use a range of devices to keep them at bay, that they hang bars of soap on their shrubs or put helium balloons with scary faces in their fields, or that some communities actually go so far as to hire professional hunters and stage one-day massacres.

And yet it is still magical to meet a deer in *his* context. Most of the time, I only realize afterward that I have been in the presence of a deer. I hear the rustling of a large animal, or I see a beige blur or the white underside of a tail flagging through the trees. Sometimes I'll be on the water and several will cross to the other side of the stream, or a doe will bring her fawns down for a drink.

These are special moments, but not so memorable as the times on the fisherman's path when I have come face-to-face with deer. Early one morning I walked down to the club's lowest stretch. I was stooping in a tiny clearing beside a copse of maples, examining a yellow butterfly, as I recall, when I looked up directly at a doe, or maybe a young buck.

Standing at the edge of the trees about thirty feet away, the doe looked at me with soft, moist, bottomless black eyes. She wasn't frightened; she seemed to be as curious about me as I was about her. With short, halting steps, she slowly closed the distance between us until she was almost near enough to touch. She stretched her neck toward me, tilting her head slightly in a questioning manner. She brought her ears forward, as if she were trying to hear what I was. Then she raised her muzzle and sniffed the air, learning nothing—or, perhaps, I thought, everything she needed to know. She started to browse the grass.

I couldn't believe the stillness, the unreality—or was it higher reality?—of the moment. It was extraordinary enough that the deer had not bolted at the sight of me, but she had, I could not help feeling, truly looked at me. Maybe it's all the literature I've osmosed, the Wordsworth and Emerson and Eiseley, but I felt as though I were standing at the border and looking across at an emissary from another world. In fact, when the deer went back to eating, as if coming upon me in the wild were nothing special, I briefly entertained the idea that I had crossed over.

I say *briefly*, for still sitting on my haunches, I became aware of a vague discomfort. I shifted my weight just slightly, and the deer was gone. She melted back into the woods, leaving me to wonder whether I had seen her at all.

Some months later, I had another encounter—this one on the South Branch itself—which lingers in memory as a companion piece to that of the deer. It was late in the afternoon on a warm early autumn day. I had been fishing for several hours and had little to show for it. But it looked like my fortunes were about to change. I had worked down to Stony Brook, where a hatch of large dark flies was developing; every now and then a trout would breach the surface with one of those delicious, slashing rises that suggest they will soon be feeding with abandon.

I moved in behind my father's rock and prepared to fish down into the guts of the pool. I was peering through my fly box, searching for an Isonychia nymph, when I heard a noise from the other side of the pool.

Looking over at the far bank, I saw a small yellow shape thrashing about in the scrub. A duckling, I thought, judging from his size, and he's in trouble. I watched the duck pull at something, a branch or root that must have had him tangled. I returned to my fishing. I tied on the nymph, then just stood there. I couldn't bring myself to cast.

A morality play started up in my head. Do I fish the pool, or do I go over and see if I can help? If I go over there, I spoil the water. It may not be fishable again for an hour, and by that time the hatch will almost certainly be played out. To make matters worse, the duckling was just below the place where the current sweeps past a big shrub that hangs over the water—the sweet spot of the pool, which I had been thinking about for the last three hours.

Maybe I'll fish the pool first, then go help him. That way, I thought, I could have my fishing and my conscience too. Or could I? I looked over at the duckling again, and I saw that he was struggling with less conviction. Animals are fatalists, I thought, my mind calling up images of the zebras and wildebeests on the TV nature shows. They ran and kicked to get away from their tormentors, but at some point they just seemed to roll over and give up.

I was about to counter this with some crap about how we all had to go sometime, how the carcass would feed other animals—Hell, even the duckling's mother must have left him to die!—when I thought of a story by Raymond Carver, in which four buddies go fishing on opening day. Arriving at the river, they find a dead girl floating face down in the water. After securing the body to some roots with a nylon cord so she won't wash away, the men go ahead with their trip as planned. They set up camp, drink a lot of whiskey, and get their fishing in; then they call the sheriff.

That did it. I went down to the bottom of the pool and made my way slowly up the other side, past the intense vegetation where the big browns like to hold. As I drew closer, the duckling became reinvigorated and thrashed harder.

I could see now what the trouble was. He was wrapped in a cloud of monofilament. A spin fisherman, a poacher, had obviously overshot his mark and broken off his lure and several yards of line on the roots. I was lighting into the culprit with the special venom that fly fisherman reserve for hardware slingers, when I saw that the duckling had a fly—a nymph, in fact—in his tiny beak.

I took the scissors that hung from my vest and carefully cut the monofilament away. I picked the duckling up. Only slightly bigger than my hand, he lay absolutely still. Was he playing dead, or surrendering to his fate? I wondered. I turned him over and examined him, and he still didn't move. He was not all yellow, some beige was mixed in, and his head was striped. What was he—a merganser? I could feel his heart beat now against my hand, faintly but distinctly, and I started to go all fuzzy inside.

When I tried to ease the nymph out of his beak, the duckling came wildly to life. He bit my hand, catching that little fold between thumb and forefinger, not hurting but startling me, causing me to drop him in the water. The duckling bobbed back up and swam quickly and noisily for the other bank, where he disappeared into the brush.

The old Greeks were right, I think. Nature reveals herself just so much, only lets you in just so far.

Nine

HUEY AND I spent the afternoon on the Amawalk outlet, a pretty little tailrace in New York's Croton water system. We separated, as usual, upon arrival. I headed up to probe the pockets and glides above the Wood Street bridge; she dropped down to a string of hemlock-fringed pools.

After a while, I made my way back. I am, by nature, a solitary fisherman, while Huey is a social one. If she had her way, we would always fish side by side. Usually, we split the difference. I tend to get lost in my fishing, so most often Huey comes looking for me. On this day, though, I emerged from my trance and went in search of her.

I bumped into Huey on the path. She had apparently been fishing in poor luck and was clearly in a snit, although she was trying hard not to show it.

"You mean to tell me, you're pissed because you haven't caught anything?" I said. I have to admit that I was enjoying her testiness. Huey is a much sunnier personality than I am, probably a more evolved human being. So I was delighted this once not to be the one acting like an asshole.

"What about the pleasure of 'just being on the stream,' the 'consolations of nature'?" I said.

Now, ordinarily, Huey has an excellent sense of humor. But it had temporarily deserted her.

"And how many did you catch?" she shot back.

"I don't know," I said. "A few."

"You know. You *always* know." She was right, of course. I do always know. "How many?"

"Eight or nine."

"That means eight." True enough, it did mean eight. "What'd you catch them on—*nymphs*?" she asked, scornfully.

Ah, my Huey was not just a predator, but a high-toned one. The fish she didn't catch were apparently on dry flies.

"Not all of them," I replied, lamely. I was starting to fish dries more often myself of late and was feeling vaguely disloyal to my father, although he fished them himself, especially terrestrials. "I got about half on a Royal Wulff, the rest on nymphs—without an indicator."

I regretted this as soon as I said it.

"I *never* use an indicator," Huey the purist hurled back at me, as she strode toward the car.

I suppose I asked for this. I introduced her to fishing. It happened at the Gorge a year before I joined Dad's club. Huey, who reminds people of the old silver screen heroines—think Joan Crawford's eyes and Jean Arthur's companionability—was perched on a VW-sized rock. She was perfectly content, soaking in the sun and plowing through the Sunday *Times*, when I asked if she'd like to try a cast or two. She tried it and loved it, opining, as a former piccolo player with the University of Pittsburgh marching band, that it was rather like conducting an orchestra.

The next week we returned to fish in concert. I fitted her with one of several eight-foot instruments made by my father. I tied on a black-nose dace, explained that it was supposed to imitate a bait fish, and showed her how to swim it in the current, retrieve it in foot-long jerks.

Looking back as I worked my way upstream, I noticed that Huey, ever her own woman, had already discarded my instructions. She was walking the fly along the bank, pulling it through the water as if it were a toy boat on a string at the park. I noticed as well that a pair of old-timers had moved into the little falls above her. They were gesturing in her direction and appeared to be enjoying a good laugh.

It was a hot, muggy July day. The fish were sulking. Nobody was catching anything. Nobody, except . . .

"Didn't you hear me screaming?" Huey asked, as I came round the bend. She was beaming. "I caught a huge one." She held her hands a yard apart.

"How big?" I said, frowning.

Huey ignored me. She was busy recounting a struggle that dwarfed Hemingway's *Old Man and the Sea*. Alas, her tale was bittersweet, for she had uncovered the dark secret at the heart of the fishing mystery. Catching the trout was great and all. But, then, well, you had to get it off the hook, which was why she was screaming for me.

"What about the two guys at the falls just above you," I asked. "Didn't they offer to help?"

"No way," said Huey. "The trout was flopping all over the rocks, and I was trying to get a hold of it. I kept looking at those two old geezers, but they just glared at me."

I knew exactly how they felt. Upstaged.

Huey and I began a tremendous season together. She plunked down a couple hundred bucks for a rod and reel. And we loaded up my vehicle and began our Errand into the Wilderness. We fished the Raritan and the Flatbrook, the Pequest and the Paulinskill. We ranged over to the Croton, sampling the West and East Branches and clocking in regularly on the Amawalk. We drove up to the Catskills, renting a house in Phoenicia, to get to know the Esopus Creek. But the mice were doing cartwheels in the walls, so we split before the week was out. We moved on to the Beaverkill, arriving at dusk at the Silver Fox Motel, where the anglers could be seen through the dining room window, knitting the twilight.

The next morning I rose with the sun and had the long motel pool to myself. I stationed myself just below the head, where the riffles apron out, and put on a favorite searching pattern. I didn't have to do much searching. One of those great Beaverkill caddis hatches was under way and every third cast one of the little euthenasiacs, fresh from the hatchery, spritzered up and impaled himself.

I was under strict orders from Huey not to wake her before eight. But word of the killing had spread, and it was getting to be standing-room only at streamside. So I raced back to the motel, whispered trout thoughts in her ear, and returned to the water.

Another hour passed before Huey, lidded with Pirate cap, materialized on the stream. She took half a dozen fish, yawned, and called it quits. She went back to bed. "I had to stop," she later said, grandly. "It was just too easy."

I knew better. She quit because it dawned on her that the more fish she caught, the more she had to somehow coax from the hook. It wasn't touching the trout that bothered her; she liked that part. She worried about hurting them. At first, I did it for her. "Honey," she would say to me, "will you show me again how you do it?"

I must have showed her how a dozen times before I realized that I was being scammed and made her commit the dread act herself. She would not do it in front of me. So I can only speculate on her method, based on certain auditory clues gleaned from the next pool up. Her exertions appeared to be as much rhetorical as manual.

"Oh, stop it! Calm down!" I would hear her scolding, ordering the fish to quit wiggling so she could get her hand around it. "Hold still, and you'll be fine."

Other times, she seemed to go for the soft sell. "My, aren't you the pretty one," she would purr—the witch putting the whammy on Hansel and Gretel.

It became evident that Huey had her own brand of fishing, just as she had her own religion: Hueyism, an eclectic blend of Byzantine Catholic liturgy (the legacy of a Pennsylvania coal town childhood) and sacred texts by people like the Dalai Lama and Shirley MacLaine. The Huey Way of Fly Fishing parallels, in places, what the rest of us do. But mostly she seems to make it up as she goes along. She disdains fishing schools and how-to books, anything that smacks of formal expertise. She even declines to use the established angling vocabulary, but prefers to improvise her own. In Huey's lexicon, trout do not rise. They "leap" or "jump," as in "They're really jumping today." They do not strike or take a fly; they "bite," as in "Had any bites?"

Huey simply does not receive received wisdom. Take the matter of wild versus hatchery trout. Everyone knows the answer to that one, right? Wrong. I remember catching a fifteen-inch native brown and dilating on the perfection of its black and red spots haloed with white, its ebon back and buttery belly, only to have Huey interrupt: "I like the hatchery trout better. They're so *silvery.*"

What do you say to this? Or to someone who greets shiners and trout fry alike as "babies"?

In the Huey Way, the usual distinctions between game fish and trash fish do not necessarily apply. For months, she spoke of a mysterious "gold" trout "with diamonds on the side," which came readily to her artificials but clearly wanted no part of mine. Just when we thought we would have to contact the Linnean Society to offer up a new subspecies, we picked the perp out of the lineup in *Peterson's Guide to Freshwater Fishes*: a chub.

Or take the business of fishing the dry fly. Almost from the start, Huey's favorite artificial was the elk-hair caddis. She fished the elk-hair irrespective of what was happening on the water. She just liked the way it looked—like a tiny beige pup tent set adrift on the current. And she would often catch fish with it, sometimes when I was doing nothing, which annoyed the hell out of me.

I would ask her how she caught them, and she wouldn't know. Which irked me more. I mean, what was the point of my reading all these esoteric tracts by Dad's authors and loading up on expensive gear, if Huey outfished me?

"What do you mean you don't know how you catch them?" I would say to her.

"They're just there," she would answer.

"What do you mean they're *just there*?"

"I mean just there, on the line."

"Wait a minute," I'd say, getting a glimmer. "Are you telling me that you don't see the fish take the fly?"

"No, I don't *see* the fish take the fly," Huey would say. "Is that a crime? Why do you always have to analyze everything? Get a life!"

The fact is, I was getting a life. Or I was starting to.

I had bought a house, a small three-bedroom colonial, white with dark-green shutters, in Bloomfield, the mostly blue-collar town next to Montclair, where Nicky and Sam lived. Now, the kids and I were not on top of each other, and they could bring friends with them to spend the night. Sam, in fact, had already become the hub for a handful of little girls on the street who seemed to call every few minutes to be updated on her estimated time of arrival.

I had made my peace at work. I had stopped blaming the place for my failure as a writer, for my inability to write anything with a shelf life of more than a week. The editors seemed to actually want to work with me again.

More importantly, I was back with Huey, determined this time to give our relationship a legitimate chance. I had been torturing Huey for going on five years. Why she put up with me, I don't know. You'd have to ask her why she did, although I am not sure that she could tell you either.

Huey is different from me. She would experience life, while, as she says, I would analyze it. Where I tend to try to drive life into a corner and hobble it, force it to open its mouth and show me its teeth, Huey lets life wash over her, bathes in it, allows it to take her where it will, never doubting it will take her where she wants to go.

Huey has no guilt, few regrets, little self-doubt, no apparent fallout from original sin. Although her career paled next to mine, by any objective measure (degrees, possessions, salary), she acted and talked about her life as if it were a huge success. "Happiness is a kind of genius," says Colette. And I think she is right. You are pretty much either born with it, or you're not. For me, being with Huey was like sitting in front of a tank of tropical fish.

And yet I was forever trying to get to a place where I felt that I could live without her.

During my separation from Molly, I had pursued

Huey with a singular passion. I had been aware of her for some time. I saw her in the halls shortly after she arrived at the magazine, and I remember stealing a peek at her office. It was cozy and neat, the books on the shelves either Russian novels or New Age classics by people like Scott Peck and Edgar Cayce. The walls were decorated with pictures of rock stars, but the place of honor was accorded to Pittsburgh baseball immortal Roberto Clemente.

We worked together for the first time on a story about a fourteen-hundred pound man. The world got wind of poor Walter Hudson when he slipped and fell on his way to the bathroom. He got stuck in a doorway, and the local fire boys had to come, saw away the wall, and pull him out.

Huey traveled to Hudson's home in Long Island and spent a day with him, then wrote a "file," from which I was charged to concoct a finished story. She talked to Hudson and his family and got strong quotes, plus the usual raft of voyeuristic details (the poor guy emptied his bowels just once every two weeks). But there was another, and unexpected, dimension to her reporting. She found a spiritual quality in this great pile of flesh.

"People who weigh a lot usually stink," Huey told me, as we worked together. "Not Walter. He's immaculate. He has a very sweet face, and he's incredibly kind, and he reads, mostly the Bible. He's at peace with himself, you can feel it when you're around him. He's a natural Buddhist."

I pursued Huey for six months. She finally gave in and returned my attentions when she became convinced that Molly and I really were calling it quits. She went from holding me at arm's length to practically living in my suitcase. Huey traveled to Spokane with me when I did a story on a boxer who went blind in the ring, tagged along when I dropped down to the Bahamas to profile a DEA hotshot who had become a nuisance to the Colombian cartel, joined me in the Dominican Republic where I hung out with a baseball scout. I couldn't get enough of her, until my divorce came through and everything changed.

I suspect that, at bottom, I am the classic American male. I celebrate individuality and self-reliance, but I worry about acting from weakness and desperation. "Trust thyself," says Emerson. "Every heart vibrates to that iron string." It's a nice thought, and one I fully subscribe to. But it assumes that the self is a single, homogeneous entity—that there is not within you a riot of contending voices, each one purporting to speak for the self.

The short of it is: I didn't know whether I loved Huey or was merely afraid of being alone.

There was something else. I worry about coming to the end of people, especially the woman in my life. With your parents and children, you don't have this concern. They're givens. But a wife is different. You choose her.

It comes down to the fact that I was afraid to make a another mistake. I had this notion that there was a woman out there who was right for me, and that I would marry Huey, or some other Platonic shadow, and this woman would come along and I would be required to get divorced again, that I would cause great pain again for people I cared about and would suffer myself.

There was one more thing. Huey wanted a child—with me. She said that some people were made to be mothers. And she was one of them.

That might be. But I wasn't sure that I wanted to plunge into fatherhood again. I had not exactly distinguished myself the first time around, and I would be in my late sixties by the time any kid Huey and I created toddled off to college.

We would have fights and she would leave. She would storm out and take the bus back to Manhattan. This went on for years. I would check my pulse and find that I was okay. I was all right living alone.

But the absence of pain was not pleasure. Pleasure is a surge, a juicing. The absence of pain is like the color white, which is of course not a color at all, but which, after a steady diet of black, can seem like a color. At least, it can for a while.

Now, after five years of breaking up and patching up, Huey and I had reached a hopeful detente. There were fewer scenes, fewer midnight dialogues about our burdened future. I was less likely to get out the checklist and focus on those categories where I felt Huey came up short (and more likely to remind myself that I wasn't quite God's gift either). For the first time in my life, I was working at a relationship, actually putting something into it, instead of worrying about what I wasn't getting out of it.

The truth is, I didn't know what to do about Huey. And I was starting to realize that I was never going to know, not with certainty. That's just the way it was. Somewhere along the line I was going to have to do something, take a leap.

Meanwhile, we had fishing between us.

Huey's friends were skeptical. One or two thought that fishing was barbaric. Others could not believe that she really liked it; they were sure that she just did it for me.

They hadn't seen Huey on the Beaverkill, the way she waded right in among the multitudes at Cairns Pool, striking up conversations with the anglers on either side of her. Usually, she worked into the flow the fact that she was with that guy over there, the one all by himself in the riffles, craned over his line with near-tragic intensity. Invariably, within the hour, Huey would end up sitting on a rock with some new pal, discussing trout tactics.

"The guys all say they wished their girlfriends liked to fish," Huey would tell me later. "And when they see that I'm not some silly girl, you know what they do? They show me their fly boxes. That's what guys want to do when they're on the stream. Show me their fly boxes."

Huey's fly box, by the way, is a Wheatley. The artificials inside it are mostly small ones, because she believes it is easier to get the small ones out of the trout's mouth. The flies are arranged by color and on the diagonal. She thinks they look like little airplanes ready to take off.

Huey was not my only fishing partner.

On a warm June afternoon, some weeks after his fifteenth birthday, Nicky and I drove out to the club.

I looked forward to the drive with Nick. There was a moratorium on serious subjects; at least, it was understood I wouldn't be the one to bring them up. I was trying to learn to listen to my son, without rushing in and attempting to "fix" him.

In this laissez-faire atmosphere, Nicky would become very chatty, and he would take the conversation into areas where I wouldn't dream of trying to lead him. We would talk about sex, about booze and marijuana. At the moment, we were talking about his hair, which was spikey and green. He was interested in what I thought about it.

"Well, it's different," I said. "I suppose it could be worse. I mean, it could be purple, right?"

"I've been thinking about purple," he said.

"Really?"

"Laura did hers purple." Laura was his girlfriend. Pale and shapely, if matchstick thin, she wore black lipstick and nail polish and had dark circles under her eyes. She already looked like someone from the Addams family.

"You know, Dad, I *am* different."

"What do you mean?"

"I mean different from the other kids."

"Do you think so?"

"Yeah, I do."

"Don't all teenagers feel that way? I mean it's a strange time in your life, very intense. And you're very tuned into your peers, worried about what they think of you."

"I've got kind of an odd personality."

"I like your personality."

"Thanks," he said, smiling. "I've got things to say that are outlandish, and having green hair helps."

"How?"

"It kind of positions me. I don't have to introduce myself. People know who I am. In a way, it kind of wins me respect. Some people think I'm scary."

"That's a good thing?"

"Yeah, because then they don't mess with me. But you know what I like most about green hair?

"No, what?"

"It's an ice-breaker. People see you and they make some funny comment about your hair, and then you can go ahead and talk. It's a conversation starter. Like we're having this conversation right now."

I had been taking Nicky with me to the Gorge once or twice a year for several years. I hadn't gone yet with Sam and did not expect to in the near future. Sam was about to turn eight. I tended to take her places like the Bronx Zoo and Great Adventure. She had the aptitude, and the tools, I felt, to be a fly fisher. She had great hand-eye coordination, and a kind of patience you don't teach. I suspected that in the long run she was more suited to the pastime than her brother. But I wasn't going to rush her.

Nicky and I would go for maybe an hour or so, and leave at the first sign that he was getting bored. I would put a streamer on his line, as I did with Huey, and show him how to work it. But pretty soon I would see him standing on the rocks toying with the minnows, or over on the bank hunting frogs.

The Gorge was the most popular fly stretch in

the state. It really got pounded. By mid-season the
fish had seen every artificial there was, and could
probably tie most of them themselves. Nicky's
chances of catching a trout, I figured, had to be a good
deal better at Dad's club.

The club water was fished lightly after the first
few weeks of the season, and the section that I had in
mind for Nicky, just below the parking lot, was barely
fished at any time. It was beneath the notice of most
of the club members who operated almost exclusively
in the upper three pools, which were loaded with
trophy trout.

As we pushed through the scrim of shoulder-
high grasses, dogwood and willow shoots that veiled
the stretch, we spooked a great blue heron.
Ordinarily, the heron discerns your presence from
hundreds of yards away, but we got lucky. I watched
the great gray Ichabod of a waterbird take those first
few, long, running steps before launching, his neck
punched out, legs dangling, as his wings slowly and
massively stroked the air.

I looked over at Nick to make sure that he had
seen it. He had and was smiling. He had spotted
something himself. He was pointing across the stream
to the opposite bank, where a mink was slipping in
and out of the vegetation.

"See that?" he said.

I gave him a thumbs up.

We stood side by side and soaked in the sun-
shine and the smell of the honeysuckle that laced
through the streamside brush. A cedar waxwing
skimmed the water. I could hear a chainsaw in the

distance, but it didn't seem to disturb, so much as underscore, the quiet. As always at the club, I felt as though I had stepped out of time.

We stood there and took in the water. There was a plunge at the top of the stretch, with little scallops to be probed, if you wished, beneath the rocks. Then came a large boulder that jutted three or four feet up out of the element, creating a hoop of placid water before and aft. The boulder was a sort of marker. It stood adjacent to fifty yards of riffles that carried toward the far bank. This thin, seemingly nondescript patch of water harbored a secret, one that the heron and the mink were clearly in on. It was the nursery for the angling club water. It teemed with rainbows, brooks, and browns that seldom exceeded seven or eight inches in length and could be readily taken with a dry fly.

Caddis, as Dad would say, was the "ticket."

Caddis flies are remarkable creatures. Where mayfly larvae cling to rocks on the stream bottom or burrow in the muck, certain kinds of caddis larvae are master masons who construct little houses out of shreds of decayed leaves, grass stems, and bits of sand, which they cement together with a glue they can apparently extrude at will. Some caddis larvae even spin tiny nets among the rocks in the fast water, where they seine microscopic forms of life.

Caddis emerge in a different manner from mayflies. They don't drift to the surface, but shoot upward like a missile launched by a submarine. Some kinds of caddis can leave their cases and be airborne in little more than a second. And they must be really delicious, because trout go nuts trying to catch them. The trout come flying out of the water, sometimes three feet into the air; or they boil on the surface, trying to nab the insects as they emerge.

I tied Huey's favorite fly, the elk-hair caddis, onto Nick's line and positioned him at the top of the riffle. It was an ideal situation. You could stand in the ankle-high current and pitch down and across into the better holding water. The idea was that the fly would sink a little as it made its journey downstream; then, as the line straightened and began to pull tight, the artificial would be impelled to rise up through the water and skitter across the surface, preferably right in front of the feeding trout's nose. ("Fish wanted a skipping fly," Dad said in his diary.)

Unfortunately, these things always work better when you're diagramming them on the blackboard of your mind. For starters, Nicky, who, like me, is left-handed, kept hanging up in the foliage behind him. He was not yet capable of making a backcast over his right shoulder—something I had not taken into account. This was easily remedied. I just moved him more toward the center of the stream.

There was a bigger problem. While he took obvious pleasure in casting—he churned the air like he was making butter—Nicky did not know how to stop the rod on the cast, at both the ten and two o'clock positions. As a result, his line and fly tended to fall in a heap upon the water.

I thought of my father, how he stood patiently by my side all those years ago, as I tasked the water with a nymph. My casting must have been at least as bad as Nick's. How many times had Dad thought of stepping in and saying something? How many times had he wanted to give me a lesson right there on the stream? But he didn't. He must have made a decision to keep his mouth shut. He must have hoped I would somehow figure it out for myself.

"Nick," I said, after watching several more futile efforts, "you're rushing the cast. You've got to give the line a little time to unfurl behind you, and in front of you too."

I could feel him stiffen. But it was too late. I had chosen my course. I proceeded to show him how to do it, explaining what I was doing with as few words as possible. I could almost see him thinking, deciding whether to try it again, or to tell me that he had had enough and was ready to go home.

After a few, interminable seconds, he brought his rod up toward his shoulder, lifting the line off the water, and made his backcast—right into the foliage.

"Wait!" I said. "I'll get it." I threw my own rod up onto the bank and ran over to free the fly from the bush. "Try it again."

He did, again and again. His casting completely fell apart. He stopped and wouldn't look at me.

"Nick," I said, "I've got an idea. Let's try one more thing. If it doesn't work, we leave. Okay?"

He shrugged.

"I mean it," I said. "We're out of here."

I showed him how to bring his right hand into play. How, after he made his forward cast with his left hand, to give a little tug on the line with his right. How a well-placed tug would stop the line from landing in a heap and would allow the line, leader, and fly to float naturally.

On his third or fourth cast, his fly skittered across a submerged rock about thirty feet below him, and there was a discernible spurt of water, made by a rising fish.

"Nick!" I shouted. "You had a strike!"

"*Dad*," he said. "Calm down. You scared me."

"I'm sorry, Nick," I said. "But this is exciting. You've got it beat. You're going to catch a trout."

And he did. He caught a bunch of them, little browns and rainbows and brookies. And he held the fish in his hand and stared at them, longer than he probably should have before he let them go.

"Wow, Dad, look," he said, as the first tiny brook trout settled behind his boot, to catch its breath before returning to the riffle. "He thinks I'm part of the stream."

Ten

R EADER, I MARRIED HER.
    On the morning of July 21, 1994, Huey and I gathered up Nicky and Sam, and drove into Manhattan to be joined in wedlock by a clerk at the city marriage bureau.

We had both done this before, with wall-to-wall family and fanfare—Huey in a church outside Pittsburgh, followed by a party at the local Moose with a polka band; myself on my uncle's back lawn that swept down to the Rahway River—and neither of us wanted a big ceremony.

Originally, we had thought to elope. That's how nervous we were about what we were doing. We were not even going to tell anyone. But then we realized how crushed the kids would be if they were excluded.

Nicky and Sam loved Huey, although they hadn't seen her in several years. After our last major breakup and repair, she decided that parting with me was painful enough; she didn't want to go through it again with the kids, too.

A couple of days before the appointed day, I called Nicky and told him what we were up to.

"Can you bear to miss school on Friday?" I asked.

"Always," he said. He was clearly pleased. Later, Ger told me that he and Sam both were "over the moon."

In my ignorance, I thought that Nicky could be our witness. But he couldn't because he wasn't eighteen. Nor, they told us, could we draft from the people queued up behind us. It was a hot day, and I was dripping with sweat, natural and unnatural. This seemed to me a weird and unwarranted codicil and I was about to argue with the clerk who had the demeanor of a turnpike toll-taker.

But Huey went out into the hallway and button-holed a lovely fellow named Rick Miller, who was there to witness another ceremony. Rick is a professional photographer, and he ended up taking what turned out to be our wedding photos in front of the building before the soaring columns.

After the blink-of-an-eye ceremony, we wandered over to Chinatown for a late breakfast. We walked into a huge barn-like restaurant off Canal Street, where we were the only gringos. It was 11 A.M., and the place was packed for dim sum. The hostess seated us at a large circular table, where a dozen antique men and women dressed in eastern finery were already chowing down. Nicky and Sam were suitably amazed and agog.

"How do you do it?" the kids wanted to know.

"You pick what you want from the carts," I said.

"I don't think they speak English," said Sam,

referring to the dim sum maids with their steamer wagons.

"It's all right," I said. "Just point."

The kids tried spring and egg rolls, crescent-shaped dumplings filled with pork, turnip cakes and sticky rice wrapped in lotus leaves, yellow egg custards in flaky crusts. And they learned about tea and civility, about sipping it from doll-size cups and pouring it for the crinkly-faced stranger beside them who bobbed with gratitude.

We strolled a couple of blocks to Little Italy and stopped for capuccino and gelato, then headed back to New Jersey. I was having the house painted, and I noticed that Ziggy the painter and his crew had chopped back most of the shrubs, so to better get at the clapboard. My mother arrived with champagne and white roses. But I barely spoke to her. I was wired and could not sit still. All I could think about were the bushes that Ziggy had axed. I wasn't angry about them. I was sure that they would grow back. But it bothered me that they were lying all over the yard, and I guess I just needed something to do.

I raced out and started gathering the branches into piles. I dragged the cuttings out back from the front and the sides of the house, then sprinted into the garage for some twine to tie them into neat bundles, the only way the fastidious garbage men would take them. When I was through with the bushes, I started thinking about an old fence I'd recently taken down; it would be a good time to gather that up and carry it out to the street too.

Looking over toward the house, I saw my mother and my bride in the window. They were drinking champagne and smiling that ambivalent, half amused and half-exasperated smile that women reserve for certain men.

"For God's sake, honey," I heard Huey say, "it's your wedding day. Do you have to do that now?"

For several years, in discrete installments, Ger had been ceding over to me pieces of Dad's life—sweaters and shirts and pants that were too thick and itchy, or too short in the cuff or sleeves, or simply too dated, for me to wear; piles of photographs of my father in college or in the navy, or with his parents and four sisters, or with my mother and me and my two sisters at home in Cranford, on vacation in Vermont, at the Jersey shore, and so on.

I would be glad to receive these things, then perplexed about what to do with them. I would look at the photos until they had no more to tell me; I would sometimes work the odd sweater into my rotation. But, in the end, most of this stuff simply went from Ger's attic to mine.

And then, around the time that Huey and I took our leap, my mother went up to her dig and excavated a relic of true power: Dad's first fishing diary.

Distinct from the other diary she had given me, which covered Dad's final years on the South Branch, this one—a manila folder containing sixty pages of unlined notebook paper—chronicled his earliest fishing adventures. The first entry, written in green ink with a fountain pen, is dated April 13, 1935. My father was only thirteen years old, but he already had that wry perspective on himself:

> This was the first fishing I had done; by that I mean serious fishing. King, Bud, Chuck and I went down in back of Watsons' [on the Rahway River] and worm-fished. They got some. Then I got a strike and they watched me. This was the first time I had had this experience. I picked up my bait-casting rod which was laying on the bank. The fish kept nibbling. Chuck told me to hook the fish so I gave the rod a very hard pull upwards. I hooked the fish and then started moving backwards and reeling in line until I was twenty or thirty feet from the bank. They died laughing and pulled the fish up. It was a rainbow about twelve inches; the first trout I ever got.

I love this entry. I love the way it is written, slightly ungrammatical and formal, laconic and earnest. I love the way its spare effects set up the comic moment when Dad hooks his trout and, instead of simply reeling in, attempts to land it by backing up onto the Watsons' lawn.

At times, when I read this passage, and others sprinkled throughout the diary, I think of Mark Twain. I know—it's a lot to put on the shoulders of a thirteen-year-old boy. But, now and then, I get the feeling that there is an ironic intelligence lurking behind the deadpan prose.

Much of the early fishing recorded in this diary is done on the river that wound through Cranford and gave the town the nickname the "Venice of New Jersey." But there are numerous forays as well to the South Branch of the Raritan near Califon, to the area known as the Gorge.

The diary is filled with my father's misadventures. He falls in repeatedly, loses his "best fly box with most of my wet flies in it," misses fish because of tangles in his line and leader, catches suckers and carp and feels no pangs whatsoever about stomping their brains out. Most delightful of all, the early entries record my father's envy of his best friend, King Ward, a feisty pip-squeak about half Dad's size who would grow up to be a fine commercial artist: "King was using snelled wet flies and he got a few strikes and he pulled in a seven-and-a-half-inch brown on a fly. King can get them on flies."

Dad takes his first trout on an artificial late in his inaugural season as a fly fisherman. He makes no big deal about it, although he does credit the trout with being a worthy opponent. "It gave a Hell of a fight, measured twelve inches," he says, then launches into a detailed description of the imitation that did the job, a bucktail tied on a "size eight, long shank hook; body ostrich herl, with black joint and silver tinsel in middle; grizzly hackle dyed red at top of the fly." He had apparently tied it himself.

Sometime in 1936, earnest Huck Finn gives way to a posturing Tom Sawyer, or at least they both begin to take turns making cameo appearances in Dad's prose. "Went to dam at 5 A.M.," he writes. "King got another brown, damn him. I didn't even get a damned strike."

My father, in the diary anyway, becomes a prodigious cusser. One day, during an excursion to the South Branch, he and his buddies find that other anglers have beaten them up there and have had the nerve to pitch their tents beside the stream: "Camps all along the bank; it is getting too damned civilized." Worse still, "the fellers were fishing worms, damn them, and they were getting full creels." My father has been fishing flies—with minor success—for little more than a year, and he already feels righteous disdain for wormers.

At the end of 1937, his third season as a fly fisher, Dad takes stock of his progress. "I caught about 25 good fish this season," he writes. "The largest fish I ever caught weighed a pound and a half and was 15 1/2 inches." He admits that he caught it on a worm, although, he says, "I used nymphs quite a bit this year, particullarly [sic] a tire tape body one." He provides an annotated drawing of the fly.

He discusses several other patterns with which he had some luck. Then he makes an entry that betrays him, I believe, as a quintessential American. In a page-long paragraph titled "Resolved for Next Year," Dad sets out a course of self-improvement, much as Benjamin Franklin tells us he did in his autobiography: "I will fish with the method of upstream fishing. I will fish a wet up and let the line float and the fly sink about a foot or more and do the same with nymphs. I will fish more bucktails and streamers in the early season. I will try big wets and bucktails and streamers at night. I will bring a camera and take pictures of the streams. I will try to see the

Pequest, the Paulinskill, the Flatbrook, the Pompton Lake River, the Musconetcong, the Mine Brook, the Rockaway. I will throw back most of the fish I catch for the sake of conservation (besides I really don't like [to eat] them an awful lot). . . ."

It is strange, and moving, to read this sort of thing by your father, who is at once dead and gone and young enough to be your own son. It is a privilege to see this man you hardly knew in the process of becoming himself. I feel a deep affection for the intolerant fifteen-year-old kid masquerading as an adult who writes this on April 4, 1938 about a fishing trip to the Flatbrook: "The place was getting to be terribly crowded and every one of them was a bastard worm dunker. We sat around from 9 A.M. to 3 P.M., talking, eating, drowsing, cursing and drinking coffee by the gallon. We had a swell time cussing like bitches."

But this swaggering poseur is about to be shown the gate. Taking stock once more at the end of the 1938 season, Dad lists the rivers he wants to fish and the flies and tactics that he intends to use on them in the coming year. He appears to pledge a new seriousness about his fly-fishing. "King is very interested in fishing again," he writes. "Thank God. King is a damned good fisherman and while he is fishing he doesn't shit around. If there is anything I can't stand it is shitting around while fishing. Little jokes and fun are all right I guess but fishing sloppily and not giving a damn about it gripe me. God I wish that I was fishing right now. . . ."

As my father gets older, he quits cussing almost completely and the "bastard worm dunkers" drop off his screen. The diary becomes all business. Now, instead of writing about how his buddy Ridge Folk is chased by an irate beaver, he offers detailed drawings of sweet spots on the river where he caught his fish, and of the flies that closed the deal. He can still be humorous. He writes in May 1939, at age seventeen, of catching a "brownie who gave about the poorest fight of any fish I ever caught. I was so disgusted with his effort that I let him go so he might improve his technique." But, increasingly, what absorbs him is his own technique—setting problems and solving them.

These later entries are much like the entries in the other diary my mother gave me, though these are more loosely and colorfully written. Reading them was like going fishing with him. Only now, instead of angling with a local expert, I was partnering up with a precocious kid. I could watch Dad over a run of days or weeks, watch him try new things out on different streams. Prior to reading his angling diaries, I had never seen my father think before. Sometimes, and these were the most exciting entries, you could actually see him learning.

In the spring of 1940, for example, he is up in New Hampshire. He is eighteen and taking a post-grad year at New Hampton Prep prior to entering Colgate University (where I would one day follow him). He and a couple of pals are fishing the Smith River during a thunder shower and catching nothing but chub. They try everything, to no avail. "So," he writes, "I decided to hook up a chub and let him swim around." He heaves the trash fish into a deep dark hole, swims it near a culvert, and watches a "big fellow" emerge from the murk and take a swat at it.

Now that he has chummed the big trout from his lair, Dad clips the chub, or what's left of it, from his leader and ties on a large bucktail made mostly of polar bear hair. Over the next couple of hours, he lays siege to the trout, angling for it three separate times, with a half-hour of downtime between attempts, so to give the fish a chance to settle back into complacency. Each time, he essays a new strategy with a different fly until, finally, he floats his bucktail slowly through the trout's domain, barely twitching it, simulating its death throes. "The showers came again," he writes, "but I finally hooked the blasted trout. What a hell of a fight he gave. I swear that I never had such a battle. He lit out for the bottom and stayed there but we finally got him up. As I didn't bring my net we had to beach him. He was a 16-inch brookie and he had a 6-inch perch in his belly."

A few weeks later, Dad is back in New Jersey for the summer, taking the train with his hometown cronies to the South Branch. "We took the 8:58 out of Cranford. It connected with the 9:11 in Plainfield and left us in High Bridge at 10:20," he writes. "The walk [from High Bridge] isn't bad; about a mile to the stream." My father would bring a small jar of "stranglepaste" (peanut butter) and he would spread it on a head of lettuce as they walked along in their fishing togs, eating and singing hobo songs.

It is summer now and the streams are running lower and clearer, and the insects are falling from the trees into the water. My father is having his first angling experience with terrestrials, although I don't think he realizes it. It is 1940 and few Americans are purposely fishing with artificials that imitate grasshoppers, beetles, and ants—insects that end up in the stream by accident. The vast majority of fly fishers are angling with patterns that simulate mayflies, which are born and die in the water. And yet my father, I am quite certain, is fishing an ant.

As I said, he doesn't realize this. He is at the Gorge "on a bright windy day," and he is casting a small "beat-up" black wet fly directly upstream, and he is taking a slew of small brook trout. He is fishing the wet fly dry—which is to say, on the surface—and he is having his success right along the bank "beneath some low-hanging trees."

Reading this entry years later, I recognize something that Dad, at age eighteen, does not—and I recognize it in the light of what his later diaries, his coterie of authors, and my own practice have taught me. The brookies have parked themselves beneath the trees to gobble ants as they fall from the branches, with help from a cooperative breeze, and that's what they take his small black fly for.

All Dad knows, and seeks to improve on, is what works. And small black wets fished up work just fine. In fact, they work better than fine.

He has been greasing his artificial to keep it riding high and dry. But the fly nevertheless begins to take on water and sink. He lifts his line to cast upstream once more and discovers that he is tight to a fish, "a 14-inch brown twice as big as the brookies."

My father doesn't write about what happened next, not in any detail. In a way, I'm glad he doesn't.

His silence affords me room to move into the scene myself. In my mind, I see Dad standing there, knee deep in the South Branch. I see his brow begin to furrow, his eyes start to blink once, twice, three times, as his stoked-up brain begins to chew over this new information.

I see him take the artificial in hand and squeeze it to eliminate any remaining grease, then dunk it to get it good and wet. (He may even reach down and grab some mud off the stream bottom and rub it onto the fly.) I watch him cast up and slightly across, thirty or forty feet, stopping the rod high to create the slack that will allow the fly to sink.

He waits. He sees something. I'm not sure what. Maybe it's his line drawing back upstream. Maybe it's a glint in the water. Maybe the stream is low and clear enough that he can actually make out the trout, or some portion of it, see it turn and knife toward the fly, then ease back to its holding lie. Whatever, Dad tightens up and finds a keeper on the other end of the line. Forty years from this date, my father's diary will be filled with entries about rewarding days on the South Branch spent fishing ant patterns. But, for now, all he knows is: "The trout wanted a small black wet fly fished up; the little ones were on top and the big fellows were a yard back and a foot below."

It's a start.

The remaining twenty-odd pages span the summers of '41 and '42. He seems to be learning everything at once. He is learning how to read the water, to pick out the stream's erogenous zones. He talks now about "watching [the water] a while before marching in" (and I see him moving quiet as an Indian along the bank, looking for surface disturbance, but also querying the bar-shaped shadows on the bottom for the telltale blink of a mouth, a pulsating tail).

He is learning about water temperature, how the fish will start to eat at forty-five degrees and become ravenous as the thermometer climbs to sixty. (He mentions "wet-wading," and I see him in his cut-off khakis, walking the South Branch in the dead of summer, using the sensors of his bare legs to find water cold enough for trout to feed.)

He is fishing all the flies. He is trying the range of dries popular in his day: the bivisibles, fanwings, spiders. He is learning especially about working beneath the surface. He uses bucktails and streamers, mostly when the water is off-color and trout will go for bait fish imitations. But streamers, I think, do not really speak to him. They are not the minded things that nymphs and wet flies are.

He fishes the wet flies of his era—the Edson Tiger, the Hare's Ear, the Black Gnat. Above all, he fishes nymphs, which are all the rage in the outdoor magazines. He is making them himself, experimenting with recipes from places like *Field & Stream*. (I see him in his house on Holly Street, in the bedroom of his childhood, hunched over his vice, making his nymphs with tire tape and rubber band bodies, collecting bits of twigs and sand and pasting them together to form mock-caddis fly houses.)

He is learning to wield his rod, what is called "tip work"—how to tend and mend his line to stave off drag, to drift or swim the nymph as if it were a living thing. But I don't think he cares all that much about presentation in the classic sense, about elegant casting. What gets him about fly-fishing is finding the trout and figuring out what he's taking and, of course, sensing the take itself.

In this last handful of pages in this first diary, Dad begins to key in on what old Skues and the other experts call "rise forms," referring to the size and shape of the hole in the water made by a trout feeding on the surface. The idea is that, if you're keenly attentive, you can tell what stage of the mayfly the rising fish is chasing by the sort of commotion he makes. It is a fascinating subject, and my father will one day be gripped by it. Right now, though, he is only beginning to make out the problem.

"The fish was bulging," he writes, alluding to the hump of water a trout creates when it whirls to take an emerging nymph. "That was not the fish's mouth you saw [breaking the surface]. That was probably his back. You should have thrown a nymph at him instead of a dry."

The diary ends a few pages later, on June 4, 1942—the height of fishing season. I wondered why.

Then I remembered: the war.

On a recent fall day, I drove out to the Gorge with Ridge Folk, one of Dad's oldest friends and earliest fishing companions. Ridge and I had been talking about making this trip to the South Branch for some time, ever since he told me that more than fifty years ago, before they all went off to fight in World War II, my father, Ridge, and two other buddies,

Bill Ryder and Cap Hansel, had printed their names on a slip of paper, put it in a mason jar, and buried the jar by a big rock next to their old campsite in the Gorge.

Ridge and I had our own wartime history. Or, better, he played a small but critical role in my skirmish with Dad over my generation's war—the so-called Vietnam Conflict. In the late '60s and early '70s, my life, like that of many of my friends, was turned upside down by Vietnam. I was against it with everything I had and knew.

I had petitioned my draft board to be recognized as a conscientious objector. It was not something I did lightly. I felt like I was ready to go to jail, if I had to. Initially, the board turned me down, but I was appealing the decision, which was where Ridge came in. Dad suggested that we invite him to the hearing, as a sort of character witness.

My father and I had traveled full circle on Vietnam, or at least on my going there. My father was a patriot, although not in any obvious way. He would stand up for the flag, say, at a ball game, but he never waved it. He had certain bedrock beliefs and loyalty to country was one of them. He never questioned it, until I came along. Even then, he didn't, or he tried not to, until I made him.

The kitchen of my parents' home became a free-fire zone. All his life, my father would walk away from difficult emotional situations, but on these occasions, when I questioned the rectitude of our being in Southeast Asia, he held his ground and really got into it with me.

Having a son myself, I see now what was at stake for him—his patrimony, his stake in me. I can put myself in his place and see what he saw when he looked at me: a young smart-ass who was allegedly his son but upon whom he had had no discernible influence; a stranger.

This is why his decision to support my appeal to the draft board, and his suggestion that we bring Ridge along, was so moving—even to me, self-righteous prig that I'm sure I was. (I remember one Christmas giving him a bunch of Vietnam books, all of them lefty tracts, so that he could enlighten himself.)

Dad and Ridge went in to address the draft board together. Afterward, as he and I rode home in the car, my father couldn't stop laughing about his old friend's testimony. Ridge, who had been a flight engineer on a B-25 during World War II and still treasured the experience, had apparently told the judge who chaired the board that he didn't sympathize with, or even understand, my opposition to Vietnam. But he believed me to be sincere.

"Judge," Dad said Ridge had said, "I have known young Bill Plummer his whole life. He plays three contact sports. I don't think he's a coward, and I know he's not a homo or a commie. He's a good kid. He's just got this misguided notion that what we're doing over there is wrong. . . ."

For nearly two hours, Ridge and I drove up and down the cratered dirt road that tracks the South Branch through the Gorge, searching for the old campsite. To guide us, we had snapshots that Dad had included in his diary and a couple more from Ridge's scrapbooks and, of course, the imperishable ones that Ridge carried around in his head.

That may have been the problem. None of the photos were conclusive; they seemed, in fact, to compete with one another, especially with the set lodged in Ridge's memory.

"Wait, pull over," Ridge said. "There, that looks like it." He pointed across the stream to a clearing where a couple of tents might easily be set up. "No, that's not it. Well, maybe. Ah, I don't know. The rock's not big enough."

Each time we stopped, it was something different. The rock was too small or too big; it was too close to the water or too far from it. The terrain was too flat or sloped. The water was not right; the old campsite was below a bank-hugging run that tailed out of a series of plunge pools. Or it was next to a riffle that flattened into a glide. . . .

The first hour, Ridge, who has two plastic hips, would struggle manfully to get out of the car and join me on the bank and gaze across the water toward the hypothetical site. After a while, as we realized we weren't going to find it, he just leaned out the car window and looked.

"Everything looks familiar," he said with a laugh. "Then, of course, nothing does."

For most of his life, Ridge worked as a salesman, peddling heavy equipment to construction firms. He never made much money, but he was always rich in friends. At age eighty, he is still first-rate company, the ultimate sidekick. He was thrilled to page through

Dad's diary, especially to see the photos of his old camping and fishing pals.

"You know your dad was big on nymphs," he said, lingering over a shot of my father netting a trout. "We'd go through a pool with our dries. Nothing. That damn guy would come through after us and take a couple out. He'd put a piece of cotton on the end of his leader and—"

"My father used a strike indicator?" I said. "Really?"

"Sure, we all did—at the beginning, anyway. Your father was the best fisherman I knew, better than Ryder, Hansel, Ackland, any of them. He was a natural. God, how I miss those guys. I go to a party now with Midge and it's all women. I don't have anyone to talk to anymore."

I hear people say that they have no regrets about their lives. If they had it to do all over again, they'd do everything exactly the same way. Who are these people? I wonder. And what planet are they from?

I am haunted by regret, motivated by it and the dread of it. I spend a significant portion of my life backing and filling. I pursued a doctorate in English at least partly, I believe, because I had done so poorly as an undergraduate and wanted to make up for it. I am determined to be involved in my children's lives because of my sorrow over my relationship with my father. I have spent hours kicking myself for not fighting past Dad's reserve, for not going into that cave where he lived and rooting him out. It is so like me to work at something after it is too late.

A couple of years before his death, my father had a stroke. I remember him lying there in the hospital bed, a slight grin on his face. He was embarassed, I think, more than anything. Most men I know learn early on not to display anything that looks like weakness.

Was he frightened? Did he sense that his days were numbered? Or had he come to some new understanding about what he was doing here on this spinning ball of dirt?

I don't know what he was feeling. I'll never know, because I never asked him. And, yes, I regret it.

I was wrapped up in my own little round. That had to be part of it. But there was another part. None of us in the family wanted to believe that Dad was in real danger. My father was a rock. We never sought to know his feelings. At some level, I think, we didn't want him to have any.

During most of my life I would phone my mother at least once or twice a week. Somewhere in the conversation I would ask about Dad, about how he was doing. And she would say, "Same as always. You know your father." When Dad had his stroke, we just wanted him to get back on his feet and head up to his barn, as if nothing had happened. We wanted life, as we knew it, to go on.

But life doesn't always go on. Sometimes life needs an overhaul or a push from a new direction.

At one point, during this period, I gave in to popular demand and went to see a shrink. His name was Alan. He used to be a bus driver and he had a weight problem, which he was not afraid to allude to. I liked him immensely. Alan told me that it was only natural that I was having a hard time. He said that I had experienced "three deaths," any one of which might have thrown me.

We worked on two of those deaths—on salvaging the remains of my marriage (my relationship with Nicky) and on getting me back in front of the typewriter (after the book I had put six years into disappeared without a trace). It's funny, but we barely talked about Dad, probably because I thought that there was little to explore.

In a time of need, when nothing worked for me anymore, I turned to my father. I found that the only thing I could get my mind around was fly-fishing, which was indivisible from him. My father had been a sort of anti-hero to me when I made my push toward adulthood. He had not even been that, really. He was an irrelevance, not even on my map. But in this time of loss, and of being lost, he showed me a different way to be in the world.

My father did not have expectations, at least none that I was aware of. Or if he did, they were absolutely minimal and of things that were within reach. And because of this, he was seldom disappointed and therefore easier on the people around him. Much of the time, you would not even know he was there.

He felt no need, no obligation, to shine. He happily hid his considerable light under a bushel.

He had no fancy notions about what he did for a living. I never heard him talk about having to feel "inspired" to turn out the work his customers called "art." He clocked in every day.

He was not afraid to make a mistake. And he

made plenty of them, as the young men who worked for him will gleefully tell you. His blunders would often be followed by great displays of temper, with chairs or crockery flying out of his shop. But he did not let his mistakes stop him from putting himself in a place where he might foul-up again. Mistakes, he knew, are the fee for learning, the price of wisdom.

He was a hedgehog, not a fox, with just one idea in his pouch. But it was a pretty good one. "Pursue, keep up with, circle round and round your life," says kindred soul Henry Thoreau. "Do what you love. Know your own bone: gnaw at it, bury it, unearth it, and gnaw at it still."

He was an optimist, I think, in the way that a fatalist can be one. By this I mean that he trusted in the rightness of things. He did not ask himself questions for which there might not be answers, the kind that render you incapable of functioning at a comfortable level in the given world.

He had a kind of selflessness. It was not that he was generous or thoughtful. He wasn't, actually. My mother is the generous, thoughtful one in the family. Other people's needs, in fact, would have to be brought to his attention, probably because he had so few needs himself and was not tuned to perceive them in others. No, he was selfless in the sense that he forgot himself. In the sense that his self was absorbed by the thing that interested him, by problems of the kind that cropped up in fly-fishing.

I found that I was willing to throw myself into fishing without worrying whether I was perfect. It was a revelation to me. In writing, I was afraid to give an idea its head and see where it would lead. What if it led to a dead end? But, under Dad's tutelage, I was beginning to think there are no dead ends in writing, any more than there are in fishing.

The important thing, I learned from my father, was to find your own bone and sink your teeth in it.

I felt like I might be ready to try to write again.

It is a couple of days after the outing with Ridge, and I am back on the South Branch. I am at the angling club, down below Stony Brook, and I have caught a good fish, a bruiser of a brown trout with white scars on his dark back and a healed-over hole near his head, suggesting that he once tangled with a heron. I am excited about catching the trout, but am not quite sure what to do with him.

I took the brown with a small gray nymph on a long tapered leader. It is surprising that he bothered with such a tiny mouthful, even in fading light. Usually, trout of this size feed in the dead of night and almost exclusively on other fish.

I took him by the club's lower limit, at the top of a small run as it bends and deepens around an island. Trouty-looking water that I've fished many times. But it occurs to me that I've never caught anything here before, not even a chub.

Kneeling in the shallows, rocking the big trout in a cove of quiet water, I realize that I have never taken a fish here because there are no other fish. Because the carnivore in my hands has eaten every piece of meat that has ever even floated through here. He has cleaned the place out.

I know that I have to kill him.

That's what a responsible angler would do. The big brown has got to be eight or nine, maybe even ten years old, past his spawning prime. He is not going to hook up with some female and pass his amazing genes along. I have to kill him for the good of the fishery. Half a dozen smaller trout will move in; the run will become productive again.

I turn the fish in my hands, and notice that he is not as big as I thought he was. He is stunted, all head and shoulders. After that, he sort of disappears, like a gymnast.

If he lived a mile upstream in the trophy pools, where the club members feed the trout by hand, he wouldn't look like this. But, then, I realize, he wouldn't still be among us. He would have been caught years ago, gutted, floured, and peppered, cooked over high heat in an iron skillet.

Perplexed, I turn to my father. What would he do? And, to my surprise, I hear my mother's voice. I hear Ger saying that Dad would sometimes come home from the angling club and tell her, "I caught my old friend again today."

This is sentimental clap-trap, and I know it. And I know that Dad knew it—he was under no illusion about what goes on between fish and fisherman. It's the sort of thing an angler says to his wife or someone who doesn't fish.

But I have no armor against it.

My father's image bodies up, as if from the element itself. It's nine or ten years ago, and Dad is wearing his favorite, beige fishing jacket and that funny green felt hat. He is down at the bottom of the angling club water, and he is releasing an eight-inch brown, not a native, but a stocked fish that will live to grow bigger and wiser.

I release the trout, too.

I revive him in the shallows for close to half an hour. He gets so used to my holding him that he doesn't try to get away, even after I loosen my grip.

Finally, I give the trout a nudge and watch him disappear, slowly and stately, into the deep, taking with him my hope that he survive another winter.

"See you," I say, "in the spring."